I absolutely love this book, and *Gain the Unfair Advantage* is a book you absolutely need to read. If you are the owner of a small business, you will be amazed at the powerful information contained in this book.

Robert G. Allen,
New York Times bestselling author, public speaker, and mentor

Gain the Unfair Advantage is a great book that inspires business owners to reach their financial potential thru efficiency, creativity, and proven strategies. It is a very sound business model to help self-employed and entrepreneurs become more successful in today's increasing competitive market.

Sam Abed, Mayor of Escondido
President, Founder,
Pacific West Consulting

AJ is my friend and mentor. His new book *Gain the Unfair Advantage* is perhaps the most brilliant business book ever written. Would you like to double your income and make more money in the next twelve months? Then this book is a must read. I am so proud to have this book as part of my library. I have read it three times and it has taken me to new heights—and I am sure it will do the same for you. After one personal session with AJ few months ago, he customized an incredible closing for me for my one-day workshop. It generated an unbelievable one hundred percent. AJ is a brilliant marketer and strategist; if he chooses to work with you, don't miss the opportunity.

John Lee
Investor, speaker and author of
Secrets of a Deal'ionaire

AJ Rassamni is a personal friend of mine, and mentor. AJ's book gives you all the knowledge you need to Gain The Unfair Advantage over your competitors and it is a must read for any small business regardless of the industry. According to US Census Bureau over 99% of businesses are small businesses. This book will show you how to automate and systemize you operation and position your company, create culture, increase profit and much more.

Jerry Yang
2007 World Series Poker Champion
Author of *All In, From Refugee Camp to Poker Champ*

I ABSOLUTELY LOVE this book! AJ is so inspiring! I have highlighters going, post-it notes on the sides, and feedbacks on the margin. It's like graduate school all over again!

Diane Phakonekham
Executive Director
Big Brothers Big Sisters of Central California

AJ, you are proof that the harder you work the luckier you get. The chances of being successful at anything by doing only one thing well are very low. All businesses are multifaceted and require owners to manage every aspect of their business and personal life to succeed. This book gives readers a road map to bring their businesses to new levels.

Anthony Analetto
President, Equipment Division
Sonny's - The Car Wash Factory

A must read for those who are looking for some simple, easy-to-follow systems that will help you take your business to the next level. AJ understands that practical solutions lead to greatness, and his way of thinking is a powerful combination of business information and common sense that will make a difference for any organization!

Brett Overman
Chairman-National Disaster Solutions

AJ, I really enjoyed reading your book "Gain Then Unfair Advantage" especially the idea of "wow factor" and the laser focus on putting customers first. I have practically highlighted or bookmarked every single page of my Kindle. You have a unique ability to explain abstract ideas in a simple and direct fashion. I now have a much better understanding why Peter Drucker said the purpose of a business is to create a customer.

Jeff Chen
Senior Financial Planning Analyst at
Brown Remus Foxworth

GAIN THE
UNFAIR
ADVANTAGE

INGENIOUS STRATEGIES FOR
EXPONENTIAL BUSINESS SUCCESS

GAIN THE
UNFAIR
ADVANTAGE

INGENIOUS STRATEGIES FOR
EXPONENTIAL BUSINESS SUCCESS

AJ RASSAMNI

Money Maker Academy
Innovate! Automate! Educate!

Gain the Unfair Advantage

Ingenious Strategies for Exponential Business Success

The Eighth Principle to Gain The Unfair Advantage

To reward you for taking the first step by purchasing Gain The Unfair Advantage, AJ Rassamni, the author is extending to you a priceless workbook to help you apply the ingenious strategies you will learn from this book to grow your business exponentially.

To download the workbook, with 251 questions to mastermind your work-plan go to GainTheUnfairAdvantage.com/priceless-work-book

I too, can be extremely successful if I have the right ideas, plans, resources, knowledge, talent and good help. Isn't that the way you feel?

This book has vital information I have collected over twenty-seven years from research, reading, attending seminars, and meeting successful entrepreneurs. I have taken their experience and most of their innovative ideas and implemented them into my own businesses for proven success. This book is filled with what I call "Wow" information that will open possibilities you never knew existed. It will give you the motivation to find the burning desire within you to take drastic measures needed to create the destiny you deserve. Unfortunately that is not enough.

I learned many years ago that life is not only about what you know, but whom you know and who knows you. What usually prevents people from breaking out of their comfort zone? It is the fear of the unknown. I encourage you to find someone who has achieved success beyond your wildest dreams and ask them to become your mentor. Mentors can help you discover the missing link to crack the code, and can introduce you to the appropriate contacts and resources that will lead you on the path to success. They will gladly teach you their recipe for success, encourage you, motivate you, and hold you accountable. They will advise you how to avoid the pitfalls they encountered over many years of experience and enlighten you through the road of success much faster than you ever believed possible.

Dedication

This book is dedicated to my wife, Sharon, and our two sons, Mark and Alex. You are the purpose of my life. I love you. I hope one day you achieve all your dreams and goals.

Success is not an accident; it is a definite plan put into action.

Table of Contents

FOREWORD

In my profession, I do a lot of traveling. I meet a lot of people. In January 2013, during one of my speaking engagements, I met AJ Rassamni. As we talked, I knew that AJ stood apart from most of the audience members. From his personality, I could tell that we had many common interests and I was intrigued to know more about him. As the year passed, and our interaction became frequent, I have grown to know AJ for the person he is. Needless to say, we have become best friends. I want you to know how powerful his brain is. He is a businessman like you would not believe. Any small business in the world that wants to learn how to increase their business, should read this book, *Gain the Unfair Advantage.*

AJ has a great story that everyone should know and learn from. When AJ was eight years old, his dad was diagnosed with cancer and died at age 42. When AJ turned twelve years old, a civil war erupted in his country, Lebanon. He endured nine years of a terrible war that tore the country apart. An interesting thing happened to AJ at that time. During the war, he learned of many people who immigrated to the U.S., who worked hard, succeeded and lived the American Dream. He grew up believing in the American Dream. AJ told me that all immigrants come to America for one reason, and that is to live the American Dream. Yet the average American does not even know that the American Dream exists. Children are programmed by their parents, schools, and by society to study, get an education and work for a reputable company until they retire. I personally don't know of any person that became a millionaire by working at a company and saving his money, do you?

AJ has studied the leadership style and the secrets of success of over 456 fast growth companies. He has taken this knowledge and applied it in his own life/business to gain the unfair advantage.

AJ writes about the recipe of success, which he devised into seven principles. The Vision Principle, the first principle you will learn from this book is how to create in your subconscious mind the conviction of success starts with the burning desire to succeed and develops into a vision and a plan. AJ is living proof of this theory. He came to America with one hundred dollars in his pocket, a burning desire, and a definite plan to live the American Dream. Nothing happens by accident, and you are in charge of everything that happens around you. This Vision Principle is the foundation of anyone's success.

The second principle, talks about the intangible secrets of success. How to surround yourself with the right network of people and mentors, and build a culture that inspires everyone around you to achieve a common goal.

The third principle is how to turn every situation into a Win-Win solution. AJ says win-win is not a compromise, and it is not, "I'll give you this if you give me that." It is much greater; it is about having the other person's best interest in mind.

The above three principles are intangible qualities that cannot be copied by watching other successful people or businesses. However, AJ captured these virtues and writes them into simpler words to learn. These mindsets are only the starting point for success.

In the next three principles, AJ writes about diverse strategies and ideas to grow business exponentially. He has a proven track record of increasing business revenue up to 100 percent in thirty days. Over the past twenty-seven years, AJ bought and sold many businesses and consulted in many others. He can walk into any business and within five minutes, find the challenge and advise how to increase profit immediately. He explains how to think differently in operating a business, how to market strategically, and to stop hard selling and start heart selling. When you push for a sale, you are actually pushing people away. Instead, AJ teaches how to become the *lighthouse* and attract fortunes. He educates on how to stop selling and use alternative strategic approaches to close more sales, more often at a higher price bracket.

The seventh and last principle is how to think like an entrepreneur and see the bigger picture, to think outside the box in order to monetize, create multiple streams of income, and take your business from local to global. This can only be accomplished successfully once the first six principles are learned and applied.

I absolutely love this book, *Gain the Unfair Advantage*, is a book you absolutely need to read. If you are a small businessperson you cannot believe the powerful information that is in this book. I want you to know that AJ is incredible, he's fantastic, he is amazing and I totally vouch for him. If you've read any of my books, which talk about entrepreneurship, this is the guy to teach you how to market your business like nobody else can do it. So read it and let him teach you exactly how to do what you need to do.

Robert G. Allen, author of the New York Times bestsellers:

Creating Wealth
Nothing Down
Multiple Streams of Income
One-Minute Millionaire

THE 7 MINDSET PRINCIPLES OF SUCCESS

The Vision Principle

Start by unlocking your potential and find the burning desire within you. Without that fire you will lack the motivation to achieve your dreams. Learn and implement the six principles that follow, apply them to your life in order to succeed.

Write your goals down and review them a few times a day. Use law of attraction, envision that you already achieved your goals, see it and feel it. Find someone who already achieved way beyond your goals, have them become your friend and mentor. Ask them for the recipe of their success and all the ingredients. Find out what price they had to pay—in money, stress, family, time, and leisure—to achieve the success you desire. Ask yourself, "Do I have the burning desire within me to pay the price of your success? Are you willing to dedicate all the time necessary to achieve these results? Do you have the burning desire to reach the fame and fortune you were born to attain?"

The Leadership Principle

Every day is an opportunity to grow your mind, heart and soul. Have your family buy into your goals. Find a new network of friends who share your same dreams and inspiration. Empower everyone around you to succeed. Assume responsibilities from others and volunteer to do what everyone avoids doing. Create a fun environment. Work and serve everyone around you better than anyone else. Work at least one percent harder than anyone else and become the star of your workplace. Become the most valuable person at work so that the business does not function the same without you. Collect contact and email information from everyone you meet.

The Win-Win Principle

Always look for win-win solutions. You are in charge of everything that happens around you, including the end result. Actions and decisions you make are to achieve your ultimate goals. Failure is not the opposite of success; failure is only the stepping-stone to success. Never take it personally, keep the end goal in mind, look for win-win solutions and become a problem solver. Challenges you encounter through your journey are only tests to find out if you are worthy of success.

The System Principle

Question all your previous beliefs. Read and learn something new everyday. Be proactive, innovate and implement new ideas on a regular basis. Automate your system where possible. Delegate your daily to do list and work on your business instead of in your business. Measure your system productivity to quickly identify potential limitations and work on solutions.

The Strategic Principle

Become the lighthouse that others look for. Stop looking for money, have money come to you. Money is the end result not the purpose. Be different. Think differently and act differently. Become the expert in your market. Fall in love with your clients and become a consumer advocate. Look at the future value instead of today's cost. Give, in order to receive. Operate at a higher standard and for greater rewards. Use technology to your advantage and implement innovation.

The Tactical Principle

Master the art of using pain and pleasure emotions as a negotiating skill. Work with passion. Master the art of human behavior to influence, and tone of voice to motivate your listeners. People must like you and trust you before they are willing to do business with you. Use closing techniques of scarcity and urgency to get customers' commitment faster.

The Entrepreneur Principle

Monetize your system and create residual income. Wake up every morning richer than the night before. Turn your hobbies and passions into multiple streams of income. Transform your local thinking to global profit.

SECTION I
THE VISION PRINCIPLE

CHAPTER 1

Lighthouse

What if you are in control of whatever happens in your life? What if you have the power to create the future you deserve in your personal and business life? What if you can stand above all and become the lighthouse that everyone is dependent on? What if instead of going out in search of wealth, you become a magnet that attracts fortunes? I am here to tell you to stop looking for money and become the lighthouse that draws riches. Throughout this book you will learn how to shift your way of thinking to attract all the wealth you deserve in your personal and professional life.

There are four ways, and only four ways, to increase profit exponentially. As I tell all of my clients, "The money is in your parking lot, you just have to learn how to get it by learning the Seven Enlightened Principles of Success to gain the unfair advantage."

Since 1997 I have purchased, consulted, and managed many businesses. In many cases I increased dollar per transaction and revenue 100 percent in thirty days. I have a proven record for increasing a business' dollar per transaction 214 percent in one day, 400 percent in one year and over 1000 percent in three years.

Although improving the closing ratio and increasing the sales dollar per transaction are the fastest methods to increase a business' revenue, they are not the only means. Increasing client base is also possible during a recession. Controlling operational expenses, eliminating bottlenecks and increasing labor productivity are other examples. While reading through this book, you will learn about the strategic and tactical levers used to increase your profit potentials and how easy it is to implement if you think out-of-the-box.

Since 1989 I've dedicated my time on the topic to reading countless books and summaries, listening to audio books, attending seminars, researching and finally implementing everything I learned by asking the questions, "How can I use these ideas I just learned?" "How can I combine the new idea with everything I have learned to gain the unfair advantage, to attract wealth and prosperity?" Everything I learned boiled down to seven powerful principles that can change your life as they changed mine.

Japan

In the 1930s, Japan decided to enter the automobile market. At that time, American autos were the best vehicles in the market. The Japanese auto industry did not invent the wheel, but they asked, "How can we improve these vehicles so we can gain the unfair advantage and dominate the market?" After performing research, the Japanese began building smaller vehicles that were better quality and had better gas mileage at a competitive price. They met with great success, and then in the 1980s, they decided to compete with German vehicles. They repeated the process and, once again, dominated the market.

What I'm trying to show is that success can be learned. Success is like a recipe with many ingredients. It is like baking a cake—if you miss one ingredient, the cake will either not look good or not taste good. The same is true in business; there are no shortcuts.

I had many "ingredients" to help me succeed in business during my journey. Some of the authors and mentors who influenced my thinking process to create the seven mindset principles include: Tom Hopkins for tactical sales, Tony Robbins for breaking through limitations, Jay Abraham for exponential marketing, Napoleon Hill for the seventeen principles of personal achievement, Steven Covey for paradigm shift, Eliyahu Goldratt for operation management, Robert Cialdini for the psychology of influence, Bill Walsh for unsurpassed business practices, and last but not least, Robert G. Allen, my friend and mentor, the author of many New York Times best selling books for speaking, writing and InfoPreneuring.

> *"Knowledge is not power, it is only potential power. It becomes power only when, and if, it is organized into definite plans of action, and directed to a definite end."*
> —Napoleon Hill

Many people see today's economy as recessionary, but I call it an opportunity. It's an opportunity to gain the unfair advantage. Take a step back and build a stronger foundation that helps reposition your business as the leader of your industry. Do you remember the reasons why you went into business? Most likely it was to earn money while providing a service. How much passion did you have? What kind of service and quality did you provide? How did you handle complaints? After establishing the business, and feeling comfortable with the income, many entrepreneurs not only forget about all the above, but also relax their services and quality because they feel comfortable that business has picked up and is in the black, instead of keeping on sweating the small details that made their business a success.

Good service is not good enough. In fact, good service is the evil archenemy of excellent service. Good enough service is expected everywhere customers go. After all, consumers deserve to get good service in exchange for their hard-earned money. The problem is that good service does not earn you customers' loyalty, nor does it guarantee they will re-patronize your business. With good service, your business becomes a convenient business. But with excellent service, you will gain the unfair advantage and become a destination business.

> "Good is not good enough.
> Good is the evil archenemy of great."

Another question: Is providing customers with good service 99 percent of the time good enough? The answer is, there is no exception for excellent service. What if airline pilots are only correct 99 percent of the time? What if doctors in operating rooms are allowed to be correct only 99 percent of the time? What if an engineer skimps on the materials used to build the foundation of a skyscraper? To gain the unfair advantage in business and succeed is to sweat the small details and provide excellent service 100 percent of the time.

Michael Phelps

There is no better story to tell than that of eight-time gold medal winner Michael Phelps and how he won the race over Milorad Cavic at the 2008 Olympics. Cavic was winning the race hands-down, but a split second decision changed the outcome. Cavic did not pay attention to a small detail. With one second left before he reached the final line, he lifted his head up to look for the wall. His head acted like a speed bump and slowed him down—that's all Michael Phelps needed to gain the unfair advantage and beat Cavic by one hundredth of a second and go on to make history. One hundredth of a second was the difference between making history and being history. I encourage you to watch Michael Phelps' interview with *60 Minutes* on YouTube.

Total Quality Management

At Boeing, as all American manufacturers, in the '70s and early '80s, it was expected and accepted that there would be five defective parts per every 10,000 parts made. Then Boeing decided to purchase parts from a Japanese company. The contract included a disclaimer accepting five defective parts for every 10,000 parts. The disclaimer was misunderstood in the translation. When the parts where ready to ship, the Japanese company sent five defective parts in a separate bag with a letter saying, "We are not sure why you needed the five defective parts. We put them in a bag not to get mixed with the other parts." Japanese companies gained the unfair advantage by having a policy of zero defects and that philosophy drove Japan to the world quality leader in the 1970s. Japan remains the quality leader; however, the U.S. has significantly closed the gap since they adopted the TQM system in the 1980s.

> *"There is no exception for excellent service."*

Only the Paranoid Survive

Only the Paranoid Survive is a book written by Andrew Grove, the retired CEO of Intel. Intel was the leader of the computer memory business, but with too much competition, Grove decided to make his exit in 1985 and concentrate on microprocessors. Every time Intel introduces a new advanced processor to the market, they already have a team trying to make that processor obsolete. Why? Because if they don't make their own processor obsolete, a competitor will. This new company will become the leader of the industry. That is what *only the paranoid survive* means. To gain the unfair advantage and be the leader of your industry, you must live in paranoia. If you stop improving and innovating, your existing customers will go somewhere else—your competitor wins and you lose.

> *"Innovation is not only mandatory, it is profitable."*

Amazon

Amazon, the world's largest online retailer, was founded in 1994 with an unconventional and innovative approach, selling books online. Then Amazon added music CDs, videos, electronics, software, toys, video games, and home improvement, which resulted in rapid growth of the company. In 1999, sales of Amazon reached 1.6 billion and *Time Magazine* named Jeff Bezos, the founder, the Person of the Year. Today, the King of Cyber Commerce (as it was called by *Time Magazine*) is challenging itself to gain an unfair advantage. They've really raised the bar for the entire industry. In 2012, Amazon introduced same-day delivery in seven major U.S. cities. The news was a shock to the entire retail industry. Rivals such as Google, eBay, and Walmart attempted to catch up, launching modest pilot programs.

Powered by "Wow" service

Don't just do more things than your competition—do better things!

Zappos gained the unfair advantage by focusing on employee happiness and offering the ultimate customer experience. Zappos employees do things out of the blue to surprise their clients. They offer extremely fast shipping at no cost and if for any reason the customer is dissatisfied, Zappos pays for return shipping no question asked.

After four weeks of intensive training program, immersing new employees in the company culture, Zappos management offers the newly trained employees the choice to quit now and receive a $2000 bonus, or continue on as an employee.

Think different

Apple's brand gains the unfair advantage upon creating innovative, high quality products. When you think of innovation in business, there is no better example than Apple. Innovation is deeply embedded in its culture; it is the DNA of the company's success. Apple dominates the market by introducing new revolutionary products to the market. There is the iPod and there is... There is iTunes and there is... Do you see a pattern?

If multi-billion dollar companies were able to recognize the need for change and continuous innovation, why do so many small mom-and-pop business owners refuse to innovate and adapt to new changes? It is important to stay hungry as a business owner. Remember the reasons you started your own business. You need to have passion to exceed customers' expectations and a sense of paranoia to innovate and stay ahead of the competition in order to have success in your market and gain the unfair advantage. Innovate or perish!

> *"The level of thinking that got you where you are today will not take you where you want to go."*

CHAPTER 2

The American Dream

In February 1985, at the age of 21, I immigrated to Houston, Texas. At that time, I did not speak any English. I went to an English learning center and three months later, I enrolled in college. I moved to California two years later. I never worked at a carwash before in my life. I was 23 years old and, like many others my age, worked during the day and went to school at night to continue my education. My first responsibilities at the carwash were at the finish line: cleaning, wiping, and delivering cars to the customers.

I was very motivated, similar to many foreigners who come to this country. Most foreigners do not come to America to earn an hourly wage, but rather to live the American Dream. I believe foreigners have an advantage over average Americans because, as foreigners, we can see all the opportunities that average Americans are born with and take for granted. Typical Americans are trained by their parents to get an education and find a secure corporate job. On the other hand, typical foreigners are raised on insecurity. I would be remiss if I were not to mention American *exceptionalism* which is alive and well in the world. Americans who see the world differently exemplify it. It is their exceptionalism and out-of-the-box thinking that helped shape this great land into a beacon of freedom and opportunity in the world.

Being raised in Lebanon, we were taught that there is no job guarantee—no one will take care of you if you don't take care of yourself, and the government will not help. Keep in mind, you have to make enough money to take care of your parents as well. When I was a kid living in Lebanon, I heard of many people who immigrated to America and became rich and successful. I never heard of anyone who failed. Isn't this a fact of life? Successful people brag about their success and unsuccessful people hide. After all, America is the land of opportunity, and I believed I would succeed like all my predecessors. After I immigrated to America, I was indeed living the American Dream. Funny thing how our brain works, if we believe in an idea our subconscious brain makes it happen. It is called the law of attraction.

After seven days of working at the carwash, I said to myself, ""Wow!" I love this business." I set a personal goal to buy the company in ten years. From that point on, I no longer saw myself as an employee, but rather as the carwash owner. It did not matter at that time how I was going to pay for it—I only had $3,000 to my name with a $200 per week income and the carwash was worth about one million dollars. I had ten years to plan and prepare. I had no clue that my goal was impossible to achieve or far-fetched for someone in my shoes. All I was doing was living the American Dream. From that day on, as I tell every business owner, I started my mornings by asking myself the following questions every day:

- What can I do to improve the business?
- What are customers' main complaints and how can I solve them?
- How can I increase the productivity?
- How can I "Wow" the customers more than I did yesterday?
- How can I increase the value we offer customers?
- How can I increase the sales dollar per transaction?
- How can I differentiate *us* from the competition?

I then brought my ideas to the owner. Within a few weeks, I was in charge of the employees' scheduling and organization. I learned how to do all the carwash maintenance and repairs and saved the company hundreds or even thousands of dollars per month by doing the repairs and maintenance myself. I would spend hours after closing doing major repairs, and be back in the morning for my regular work schedule. I learned how to detail vehicles, and eventually was in charge of the detail and front line quality control. I also took over customer complaints. When everyone else was avoiding complaints, I ran toward complaining customers. I also learned Spanish, and today my Spanish is as good as my English. At that time, I was making $200 per week and was not being compensated for the extra hours I spent at the carwash. To be fair, extra compensation was the last thing on my mind.

The general manager and office manager were more than happy to let me take over all these duties because it meant less work for them. They did not realize I was preparing to become the most valuable person in the carwash, or that I had plans to take over the entire operation and eventually own it. After a couple of months, I became the front area manager. Real job security is not when you need the work, but rather it's when the work needs you. I became more valuable than what I was getting paid to do, but that did not bother me. As a matter of fact, this is exactly how I wanted it to be. Many employees go to their boss and ask for a raise and promise they will work harder, but the fact is, you have to be worth much more than you are getting paid. The business owner will feel obligated to you and will have no choice but to give you a raise even without you asking. A successful owner knows that if he doesn't take care of star employees, then someone else will. That is what employment security is all about.

> "Real job security is not when you need the work, but rather it's when the work needs you."

I was preparing myself for an opportunity. It is better to be prepared for an opportunity and not have one, than have an opportunity and not be prepared. In 1989 that opportunity knocked at my door. A customer came in and asked to speak with the general manager (GM) for a detail quote. Since the general manager was not at the carwash, I gave her the quote. The customer did not react, but requested to talk to the general manager. So I called him at his home and handed her the phone. Two minutes later the customer left upset and the GM called the carwash to talk to me. He insulted and disrespected me, demanding that I no longer give quotes for detail work. My response to him was that if he didn't want me to do his job, then he should be here during business hours and not at home relaxing. He became furious and fired me over the phone. I responded by saying the owner hired me, and only the owner can fire me.

As it turned out, the customer had previously talked to the GM about having her car detailed and he had given her a price of $250. When she asked me for a quote, I gave her the same job for $200. So when the customer talked to the GM on the phone, she accused him of trying to overcharge her.

Just to clarify and be fair to the GM, the detail package the customer requested was $250, but we sometimes gave discount to customers to get the sale. Up until that point I was not involved in sales and had neither sales experience nor the confidence to sell such a big item, so I automatically offered the customer a discounted price. Also, to give credit to the GM, he was one of the best salespeople in the carwash industry, if not the best. If you recall, in the late '80s the average price for a complete detail was $80 to $100. We were the only carwash in town to offer a complete detail with Teflon sealant and a one-year warranty for $250. We had the best detail department in the area and the best reputation.

Within twenty minutes the GM was back at the carwash to fire me, but I refused to leave, as I knew I had not done anything wrong. The owner was overseas and was coming back in one week. A week later, the GM picked up the owner from the airport and told him his side of the story. I told him my side of the story the following day. The next day, the GM had an argument with the owner and gave him an ultimatum, "Either fire AJ, or I leave." Well, he left and I stayed. The owner called a meeting for the sales manager, office manager, and me to inform us about the GM's decision to leave. The owner's main concern at that meeting was that detail sales might drop, so I offered to help write tickets and promote the packages and detail menu.

> *"It is better to be prepared for an opportunity and not get one, than have an opportunity and not be prepared."*

My Best Investment

At first I was faced with a lot of rejections. And with no sales experience, all the rejections made me withdraw. I didn't want to talk to customers, and I didn't want to sell to them anymore because I was afraid to hear the word "no." Then someone told me about a sales seminar in town with Tom Hopkins and encouraged me to attend. The one-day seminar cost $150 at that time and my weekly salary was only $250. After the seminar, I was so excited about what I had heard that I bought his audiotapes to learn more on how to sell. The audio investment was another $150.

I took those tapes, listened to them, and reviewed the workbook over and over again. Within 30 days I was able to double the detail sales at the carwash. I was still working the same amount of hours and still talking to the same amount of people, but I doubled the sales of details and, in direct proportion, I doubled my commission. I learned a few lessons during that experience, including:

- Your sales grow in direct proportion to how many prospects per hour you educate on an existing problem and offer them solutions.
- Your sales grow in direct proportion to your ability to handle objections.
- Your sales grow in direct proportion to your ability to handle rejections.
- Your sales grow in direct proportion to your ability to close the sale.
- Your sales grow in direct proportion to how much added value you offer.
- Your sales grow in direct proportion to your service guarantee.
- Your sales grow in direct proportion to your ability to lead customers to make the right decision by asking questions.
- Your sales grow in direct proportion to your ability to listen more than talk.
- Your sales grow in direct proportion of your learning experience from every rejection you receive.
- Your sales grow in direct proportion to how many customers you offer your services to per hour.

Within six months after the GM left, I took the initiative to fill his gaps. The other two managers didn't mind because there was a lot of work and they did not enjoy the added responsibility. Then I confronted the owner to appoint me as the general manager, double my salary and give me 10 percent of the carwash profits or I would leave for a better opportunity. (Note: The previous GM was receiving 40 percent of the profits.) From 1989 to 1992, I increased the business by about 20 percent per year and by 1996, I was earning 25 percent of the carwash profits.

In 1996 opportunity knocked again. The owner wanted to sell the carwash. The good news is that since 1989, when I earned my first 10 percent until 1996, when I was earning 25 percent, I never took my shares of the profit out of the carwash. Instead the owner was withdrawing all the profits, and we kept records of the money he owed me. We estimated the value of the carwash at that time, minus my profits on the books. I still had to come up with a large sum of money that I didn't have to purchase the business.

Why wasn't I taking my profit share, you ask? As I mentioned previously, after one week of working at the carwash, I set my goal to purchase it within 10 years. From that point on, I saw myself as the owner, but did not have the keys yet. Everything I did at the carwash was to reach my goal of purchasing the carwash by January 1997.

I was unable to obtain a traditional bank loan to purchase the car wash business because I did not have enough home equity or other collateral. I almost gave up, as most people do, when faced with rejection.

Control Your Destiny

Since 1987, after I set my goal to own the carwash, I acted like an owner and a partner. I acquired new friends and all my friends from that point on were business owners. I surrounded myself with people who already achieved goals similar to mine and were already living the life I desired. I remember one of my friends (he owned three different businesses) looking me straight in the eyes and saying, "If you don't buy the carwash, you are stupid." I had another friend who offered me the equity in his house as collateral.

This is the difference between surrounding yourself with people who are entrepreneurs and surrounding yourself with people who have no motivation to improve themselves, who accept the status quo. If I had surrounded myself with employees who just worked for their paychecks, they would have discouraged me and told me I could never buy the carwash and would have killed my dream.

A great motivator once asked the question, "If you had a new idea to open a business and make a lot of money, but after you put all your money together—every penny that you have—you still needed $50,000, what would you do?" Most people would just give up because they don't have the money. But what if somebody kidnapped your child and then told you that they wanted all the money you have plus $50,000 within twenty-four hours? Then what would you do? Wouldn't you contact everyone you know to get the money together and refuse to take no for an answer? Would you have a sense of urgency that you must put the money together within that time and failing is not an option?

This is the same burning desire you should have to open a business. If you really believe that once you have the money to start a business you will be very successful, why not ask everyone you can think of to become your investor or to join you in the business venture? You'll never know what the answer is until you ask. As professional hockey great Wayne Gretzky once said, "You miss 100 percent of the shots that you never take."

I did not feel comfortable borrowing money from my friends. I had excellent credit so I called my bank and applied for a line of credit through the business. I received two lines of credit and also a second loan on my house. I came up with some creative financing and offered to pay off the remaining balance in two years.

You can achieve anything you want in life if you follow these formulas:

•   You have to know what you really want and have a burning desire to achieve it.

•   Write down your goals with specific dates to accomplish them.

•   Post your goals where you can read them every morning and evening.

•   Surround yourself with people who have already achieved way beyond your goals and have them as friends.

•   Have some of your new friends become your mentors. Invite them out one at a time and make sure to pay for lunch. Take a pen and notepad with you. Ask them to tell you their story, including details such as their personal feelings and their driving force at the time, what they had to give up to get to where they are today, how long they had to work, the price they had to pay for their success and the rewards they received, etc. In short, ask all the questions possible about their emotional, physical, and mental state and write everything down.

•   Review everything you learned from previous steps and ask yourself, "Am I ready and willing to pay the price to achieve my goals? Do I have the burning desire to achieve those goals?"

As you can probably tell by reading this book, I live by quotes, as powerful quotes have a unique way of distilling wisdom to its essence by putting things in perspective. I borrow some quotes from speakers, historical figures, or celebrities, while I come up with others on my own. Here are some of my favorites:

- "You'll reach tomorrow with whatever seeds you plant today."
- "How high you soar depends on how many people you help along the way."
- "You are who you are today because of certain decisions you made in your life and certain decisions you did not make."
- "You are where you are today because of the price you were willing to pay."
- "To get what you want in life, help other people get what they want first."
- "Do the first thing first."
- "I must do the most productive thing possible at every given moment."

I had this last quote posted in my office for many years and read it a few times a day. I learned it from Tom Hopkins and he learned it from his mentor J. Douglas Edwards.

The Law of Attraction

The ownership of your destiny begins by following the recipe of success. The first rule of the recipe to the road of success to gain the unfair advantage begins with a state of mind. You must write your goals down (do not use a computer to type your goals) and review them a few times a day. Post your goals on the mirror in your bathroom to read them first thing in the morning and just before you go to bed at night. Post them in your office where you can see them and read them a few times a day. Have your family buy into your goals. You must believe and visualize that you have already achieved those goals without a doubt. Listen to your inner voice and make sure that the doorkeeper of your inner voice is on your side and believes in you and your goals. If the doorkeeper has some negative thoughts, visualize him as an outsider and ask him to leave. (Our brain does not know the difference between reality and visualization.) Any doubt from your doorkeeper will prevent you from manifesting your destiny. Whenever you have a positive thought that is full of intensity and emotion, your brain transmits a vibration that attracts the right people and circumstances to you to manifest your desires.

No one is prevented from getting rich because of lack of capital. Feel the burning desire of what you want to achieve. Appreciate and be thankful and feel blessed for everything that happens in your life. Do not concentrate on the small, vague details that prevent you from achieving your destiny that puts some doubts in your beliefs. Allow the universe to figure out those small details for you.

Building a Foundation

Many people have asked how long it took me to write my first book. My answer is, I was reading, researching, collecting information, writing pages, paragraphs and chapters about different ideas for over ten years. Then in January 2010, I decided it was time to write a book, and I completed the book within six months. My question to you... Did it take me six months or ten years to write the book? Could I have written the book within six months if I did not have the ten years of documented research?

Bamboo Tree

Let me tell you about the bamboo tree. The first year, when it is planted and nurtured, there is no visible growth. It is the same with the second, third, fourth, and fifth years. Despite no visible results, the farmer keeps watering and fertilizing the bamboo tree. Then sometime between the fifth and sixth year, the bamboo tree grows over eighty feet high within a six-week time frame. The first five years, the bamboo tree worked on building a strong foundation to help it soar eighty feet in six weeks. The question is, did it take six weeks or five years to grow eighty feet?

Isn't this the same as in business? You must strive to cultivate and build a foundation of amazing employees who believe in your mission to exceed your customers' expectations with every visit. You want employees who buy into the idea that customers are the most important people in your business. Your employees must understand that they are not doing the customers a favor by serving them, but rather customers are giving them the opportunity to do so. It is all up to you, as the business owner, to build a foundation of amazing employees. Employees are mirrors of your business, the way you treat them is reflected back to the customers. It is called Karma.

"You are not measured by what you say, but rather by what you do."

SECTION 2

THE FOUNDATION PRINCIPLE

CHAPTER 3

Rain Drop

People ask me, "What's your secret? What is the one thing you do to increase profit exponentially and make a difference?"

My answer is this:

As you cannot blame a flood on one drop of rain but on all the raindrops combined, so too, there is not just one thing you do to grow your profit exponentially. It is all the little "Wow" moments combined that keeps clients coming back. To gain the unfair advantage you must provide an unforgettable experience every step of the way, starting with the landscape, paintings, value, greeters, bathrooms, waiting area, speed, quality, excellent customer service etc. Give customers as many reasons as possible to come back more often. Become a destination business, not a convenience business. Convenience businesses are the norm; they are a dime a dozen. Destination businesses, on the other hand, offer an experience worth every dime. How many raindrops do you use to attract new customers, increase frequency of visits, and dollar per transaction? How strong is your rainstorm?

> *"A flood cannot be blamed on one drop of rain, but on all rain drops combined."*

However, if there is one visible raindrop that contributes most to success, it's the culture you build at your business with employees. The first and most important thing I do when I buy a new business, or even hire a new employee, is conduct a lot of staff meetings and meet with my employees individually to build the desired culture. Employees, and not the business owner, are in direct contact with customers. Customers don't do business with companies; they do business with people. The happier the employees are, the nicer experience customers will have at the business.

I have two cars, a BMW and a Cadillac. The service departments I take them to are 30 minutes away from my home. I use both of these departments, not because of the respective car dealerships, but because I've developed a good relationship with the service advisors. I trust the people to take good care of my vehicles.

Since my BMW service person left the dealership, I have never been back. I now take my vehicle to another BMW dealer that is only five minutes from my business. As for my Cadillac, before the service person left he called me and introduced me to another service advisor. I continued taking my car to that dealer until the new advisor left. Since then I take my Cadillac to another dealer that is also five minutes from my business, which is more convenient.

> *"People do business with people, not companies."*

Greatest Asset

What is the greatest asset of your business?

- Is it your equipment?
- Is it your building?
- Is it your technology?
- Is it your marketing and sales techniques?
- Is it you, the business owner?

Most businesses operate under the assumption that the business owner is the greatest asset of the business and is the person everyone has to please. The fact is, customers are the most important assets of the business. Staff and employees are close second because they are the people in contact with the customers on a daily basis. The owner may oversee the operation and get to know some clients, but the employees are in direct contact with the clients every day. The manner in which the owner treats the employees is mirrored back to the way the employees treat the customers. When employees are mistreated or disrespected by the owner, it is normal human behavior that employees have no loyalty to the business. They do not have the business' best interest in mind. Therefore they will not have any reason to take care of the customers. All the employee will care about at that point is showing up to work and putting their hours in so they get paid. This is not the attitude you want your employees to have when they come to work.

If, instead of mistreating the employees, an owner builds a business philosophy based on building a culture to serve the employees, they will be happy to come to work everyday. Have the staff feel as if they are owners and create a sense of urgency that we are all in it together. In return, employees will put forth the effort to please customers and keep the best interest of the business at hand. For a business to remain successful you have to provide the highest quality and unsurpassed service in the fastest time possible to exceed customers' expectations and give them enough reasons to come back. If customers do not come back, you lose and your competitor wins.

> *"The way employees are treated, is mirrored back onto customers."*

The following chart shows the priority of importance in most businesses. Managers and employees want to serve the owner so they keep their jobs. When employees serve the owner, they forget about the customers. The problem is this way of operating, you will be missing the first cornerstone needed to build a strong foundation to grow your profit exponentially and gain the unfair advantage over your competitor.

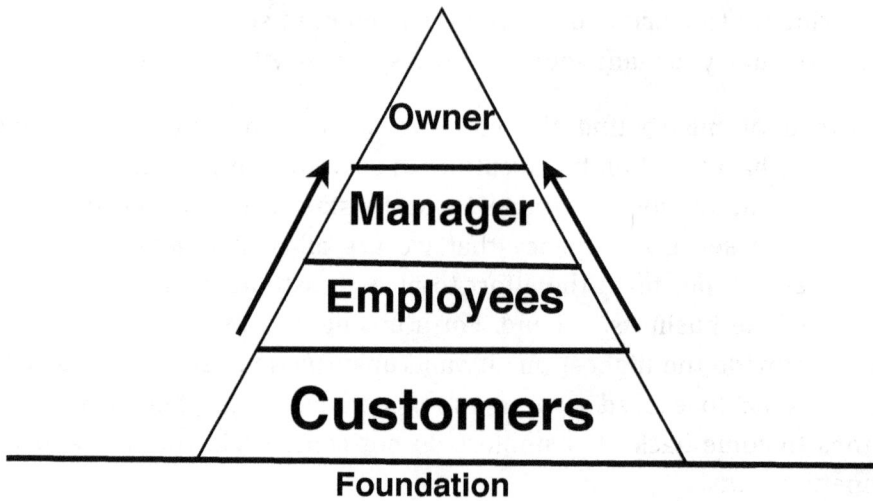

Owner
Manager
Employees
Customers
Foundation

> "Fall in love with your Clients, not
> your company."

I visit many businesses, and some of the questions I ask management and employees (excluding owners) include:

- Who is the most important person in the business?
- Who is the person you want to make sure you please so you keep your job?
- Who is the person who pays your wages?

Sadly, many still believe that the owner is the most important person everyone has to please. As many employees have said, "Because he/she is the boss and pays our wages." The only answer for all these questions is, the customer is the most important person whom we must please at all times so he/she comes back and pays our wages.

> *"If you always do what you always did, you will always get what you always got."*
>
> *A. Einstein.*

The most successful organizations are those who understand the true meaning of falling in love with the customers, not the company. The most prosperous businesses are the ones who invert the triangle and build a foundation based on the owner as the main servant to managers and employees. Inverting the triangle takes time and actions by the owner to create a culture where everyone's main concern is to serve the customer, appreciate their business, and exceed their expectations, so that the customer will remember the experience and come back.

Build your business on serving the customer and understanding that the customer is not an outsider of the business, but instead the main part of it and the main reason why the company was founded. A business philosophy based on owners serving employees is one reason why organizations prosper in good and bad times. After all, people do business with people, not companies.

> *"Great staff makes great companies.*
> *We cannot win the battle without great soldiers."*

Every single customer experience counts. You can differentiate your brand based on the experience and service you deliver to your clients. The better customer experience your company provides, the more likely your customers are to purchase from you again and to recommend your products or services to friends. These intangible experiences are hard for your competitors to copy.

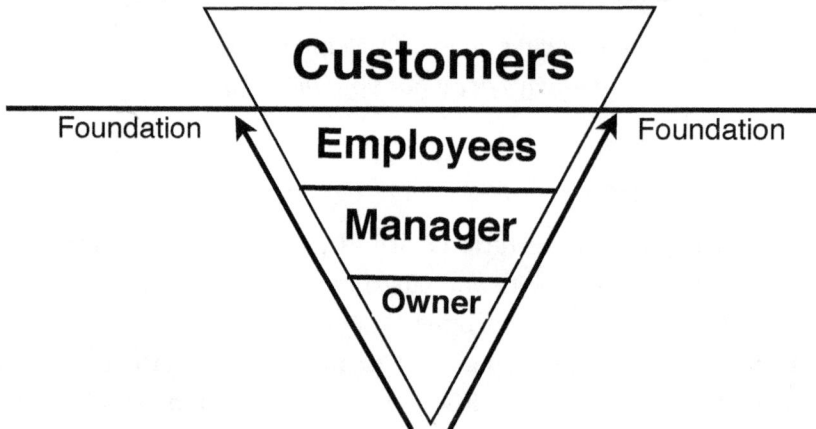

Why is building a culture important to the success of your business?

Would the following stats be good enough reasons?

- It is 6-7 times more expensive to gain a new customer than it is to keep an existing one (White House Office of Consumer Affairs; blogs.salesforce.com, Alex Hisaka on July 25, 2013).
- 78 percent of consumers have abandoned a transaction due to bad customer service experiences (American Express Survey 2011; blogs.salesforce.com, Alex Hisaka on July 25, 2013).
- Unhappy customers are highly unlikely to be repeat customers as 89 percent of customers report having stopped doing business with companies because of bad customer service (RightNow Customer Experience Impact Report 2011; blogs.salesforce.com, Alex Hisaka on July 25, 2013).
- People are twice as likely to talk about bad customer service experiences than they are to talk about good experiences (2012 Global Customer Service Barometer; blogs.salesforce.com, Alex Hisaka on July 25, 2013).
- 9 of 10 consumers say they would pay more to ensure good customer service.
- 70 percent of customers will do business with you if you resolve their complaint.

- 89 percent of consumers began doing business with a competitor following a poor customer experience. (RightNow Customer Experience Impact Report 2011).
- 2 percent increase in customer retention has the same effect on profit as cutting costs by 10 percent.
- 5 percent increase in customer retention can increase profit between 25 and 125 percent (Harvard University; hbswk.hbs.edu, Frederick F. Reichheld and Phil Schefter on July 10, 2000).

Reasons why clients stop patronizing your business

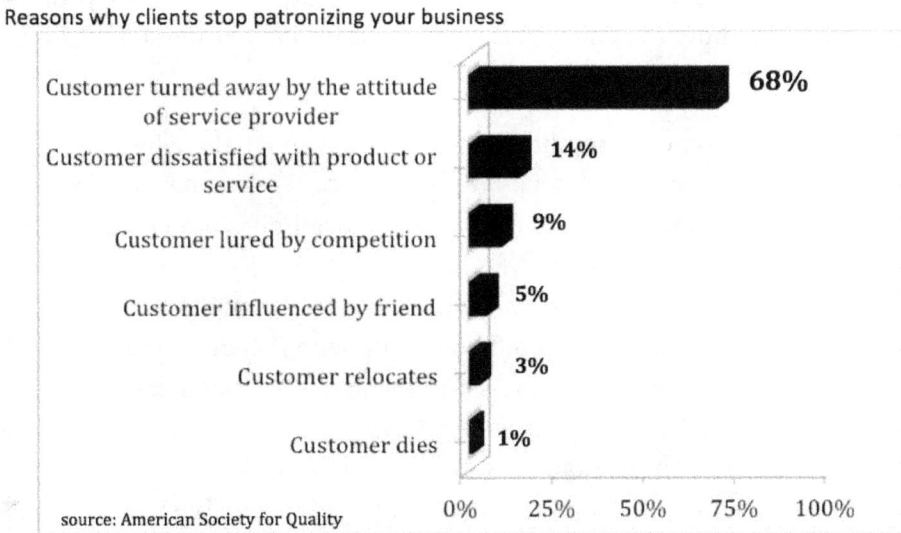

Reasons why clients stop patronizing your business

Reason	Percentage
Customer turned away by the attitude of service provider	68%
Customer dissatisfied with product or service	14%
Customer lured by competition	9%
Customer influenced by friend	5%
Customer relocates	3%
Customer dies	1%

source: American Society for Quality

Star Fish

A boy and his grandpa were walking on the beach in the morning. The previous night, the high tide washed all the starfish onto the beach. The boy asked his grandpa, "What's going to happen to all these starfish?"

Grandpa: *"If they don't go back into the water they will die."*

Boy: *"There is nothing we can do, there are too many. They will all die."*

The grandpa picked one up and threw it back in the sea.

Boy: *"What are you doing? You can't save them all."*

Grandpa: *"You are right! I can't save them all, but I sure made a difference to this one."*

The same concept applies in business. By serving and "Wow"ing one customer at a time, you can build a strong foundation of clients who become your best advertisers and who will be willing to drive by many other similar businesses to come to yours for the experience. Because of the trust you build, these same customers will be willing to purchase higher priced items or services.

Change the employees' perspectives of who's the boss. In your meetings talk about how the customer is the most important person in the business. Use any of the following messages:

- Customers are the bosses and we must do whatever our bosses want so we can keep our jobs and collect our paychecks.
- The more clients we have, the more hours we work and the bigger our paychecks will be.
- The fewer customers we have, the less money we all make.
- Our success and quality of life depends on our customers.
- Once customers leave our facility, they have the choice to use a competitor's business next time. We can control their decision if we give them enough reasons to come back.
- We need to "Wow" them so much that our business becomes their destination.
- We're in it together; let's make sure we exceed our bosses' expectations.

The only way you can achieve all of the above is if the staff are happy at work. If they come in every morning with the intention to serve the customers and exceed their expectations, that's where your job comes in. You are not their boss; you are their servant. They work for the customer and you work for the employees. Their job is to make sure the customer is happy with the service and has a great experience. Your job is to make sure the employees are happy at work and have a great experience.

> *"Deliver an amazing service to your clients and you will stand out as a lighthouse.*

If you have a choice between a work environment that is friendly and supportive and one that is hostile and discouraging, which one would you choose?

- If you want ideas to grow, the work environment must be enjoyable.
- People who enjoy doing what they are doing, do it better.
- Fun is infectious and has a snowball effect that helps breed exceptionalism throughout the company.
- There is a direct link between joy at work and employee creativeness, productivity, morale, retention, and customer service.

Your staff must be empowered to do whatever it takes to make sure customers' expectations are exceeded. Create a fun, family culture and sense of loyalty. Build a sense of urgency to do whatever it takes to exceed customers' expectations. Your common goal is to work together as a team to "Wow" the customers.

When you hire a new employee, if that person doesn't learn to become part of your culture and work as hard as everyone else, the other employees should be empowered to collectively make the decision and advise management if they want that person to continue working with the company. Like each one of your fingers is different from the other, each staff member is an individual and different from the others. Your job, as the team leader, is to have them work together as one, as you bring all your fingers together to work as one hand.

Keep in mind that it takes eighteen months to build a culture. Do not give up if you don't see a difference in a few days, a few weeks, or a few months. Employees tend to resist, challenge and push the envelope because they oppose change. You have to prove to them that you mean it and practice what you preach. It takes eighteen months to build your business culture and it starts with one starfish at a time. Remember the Golden Rule: Treat others, as you want to be treated.

Your mission statement should include the following sentence "To consistently exceed our customers' expectations and become the standard by which all (type of business) are measured."™

You must have two rules that everyone must follow:

1. The customer is always right.
2. When a customer is wrong and you know that he/she is wrong; when a customer is trying to take advantage of you and you know he/she is trying to take advantage of you; when a customer is getting on your nerves and you have no choice but to ask him/her to leave: Please refer to rule number one.

It's easy to have a win-lose or lose-win solution. It's much harder to have a win-win solution. Win-win does not mean to compromise. It does not mean I agree with you if you give me something in return. Win-win is to truly fall in love with your clients and to do what is best from them. Remember to keep the end in mind. After customers leave your business, you cannot force them to come back. The end-in-mind thinking starts with asking the question, "We are not at fault for what the customer is accusing us of. On the other hand the customer truly believes that we are at fault. Therefore, what can I do to make sure the customer leaves happy and comes back for his next service?" Note that if a customer leaves unhappy, you lose and your competitors win. I suggest you read *The 7 Habits of Highly Effective People* by Stephen R. Covey to understand the "Win-Win," "Begin with the End in Mind," and "Sharpen the Saw" philosophy.

> *"It takes seconds to lose a client, and years to earn one."*

Keep in mind that when you lose one customer, you're actually losing ten on average. The upset customer goes home and tells his spouse, kids, friends, and coworkers. Today, with social media websites everywhere you turn, you can't afford to upset a customer. The news will spread like wildfire and may cost you hundreds of customers over the years.

What happens if the customer goes home and posts his complaint on Yelp, Google, Yahoo!, Facebook, Twitter, etc.? There are possibly thousands of people who may read the complaint. What if only 10 percent of the readers believed him? What if 10 percent of those 10 percent repost the same complaint on their blogs? As you can see, the number of customers you may lose is potentially unlimited.

Why do people drive out of their way to go to Starbucks and pay more for their coffee? Is it because it tastes better? Or is it because of the experience and atmosphere?

I suggest you read the following two books about Starbucks: *Pour Your Heart Into It: How Starbucks Built a Company One Cup at a Time* and *It's Not About the Coffee: Lessons on Putting People First From a Life at Starbucks.*

FYI: A happy Starbuck employee invented one of Starbucks' most desired drinks, the Frappuccino.

Start with Your Why

When business owners are asked what differentiates their business from the competitors, many answer by saying it is their friendly service. Some may say they offer fast delivery or lower prices. Though all of the above may be important to run a successful business, they are not enough to differentiate one business from the other because these benefits can be easily copied. Building customers' loyalty takes more than a few features and benefits. It is about the whole experience. It is about looking at your business from a different perspective. You are not in the business to provide a service or a product, you are in the business to solve a problem, to create happiness and make customers feel good. It starts with the "Why" are you in business. Every business owner is in business to make money, which is the end result. This is not the "Why" what we are talking about. This is about the inner "Why," your own vision, your purpose that inspires you, your staff and your customers to care about your company and become loyal to your cause and brag about your business. Why do some clients drive by other similar businesses that may provide a better and faster service or product at lower price just to come to your facility? What makes them connect with your business and become raving fans?

Apple® owns 6 percent market share of computers sold worldwide. Yet 35 percent of all money received from computer sales belongs to Apple. As a matter of fact, Apple sells over 90 percent of computers that are sold costing over $1,000. Apple created a brand that is second to none. It has raving fans that are willing to pay three or four times more to buy an Apple brand versus a competitor brand.

Simon Sinek, in his book *Start With the Why,* said it best in an example about Apple. He said, "Apple is just a computer company; they have the same access, the same talent, the same media and the same pool of customers like every other computer company. Most computer companies promote their business by saying something like, we make great computers, they are beautifully designed, simple to use and are user friendly. You want to buy one?" That is how most companies including carwashes communicate. Most carwash operators for example promote their business with a similar message by saying, "We provide a clean, shiny and dry car; do you want to wash your car?" The message works but it does not differentiate you from your competitor.

Simon Sinek explains that Apple communicates differently. They start with their "why." They start by sharing their beliefs, their purpose and their cause by saying something like, "Everything we do, we believe in challenging the status quo, we believe in thinking differently, the way we challenge the status quo is by making our product beautifully designed, simple to use and user friendly. We just happen to make great computers; do you want to buy one?"

Notice, basically the same words were used in both messages. Except, Apple started with its belief that inspires them to do what they do. Which one sounds better to you? What computer company are you more comfortable buying from? To create your business brand, start with what inspires you and others. Start with your inner "Why," your vision, your purpose and your cause.

Dedicate your time to promoting your cause, and since it costs up to nine times more to gain a new customer versus retaining an existing customer, invest in tools that will help you target the right message to the right customers to earn their loyalty and keep them coming back more often.

> *There are leaders and there are those who lead.*
> *Leaders hold a position of power or influence.*
> *Those who lead inspire us.*
>
> *Simon Sinek*

CHAPTER 4

The Treasure Map

July 2007, at the peak of the recession, I purchased a carwash in California. Here's a brief history of the carwash: The carwash was built more than 50 years ago. Since then, the development has moved north and the traffic count in front of the carwash has gone down from forty thousand cars to twenty-nine thousand cars. In 1990, the landlord remodeled the carwash and ran it for two years before selling the business with an option to purchase the property. As a matter of fact, the carwash was re-sold at least four different times by the owner between 1997 and July 2007 when I acquired the business and immediately exercised the option to purchase the property.

I will explain my thinking process and many of my actions. I'm going to tell you how I was able to increase the business by 1000 percent in three years, during the recession, while other carwashes and businesses in general were down by as much as 50 percent during this same time span.

Here are more quotes I live by:

- "An unexamined life is not worth living." — Socrates
- "If you fail to plan, you are planning to fail." — Benjamin Franklin
- "Innovation is not only mandatory, it's profitable."
- "Change starts from the foundation and a blueprint."
- "You can modify your future's past by doing what you wish you did."
- "If you continue on doing what you've been doing, you continue getting what you've been getting."
- "The level of thinking that got you where you are today will not take you where you want to go."

Think of an architect who wants to build a house. What are the steps he takes?

- He asks many questions regarding requirements (i.e. square footage, number of bedrooms and bathrooms, the directions bedrooms are facing, square footage of each room and so on.)
- He draws the blueprint according to requirements.
- He starts building from the foundation up.
- He builds a strong foundation with many pillars to support the house above.
- He builds the house to specifications.
- He furnishes the house.
- Finally, he invites people over for the grand opening.

Business Plan

Those are similar to the steps I have used:

- **Discover**, perform your due diligence before you commit to invest your hard earned money. There are many areas to discover.

- **Observe the business** for neatness, employees, business process, product quality, bottleneck, time it takes to serve a customer, signs, bathrooms, waiting area, equipment, etc. Speak with employees and even take some key workers to lunch one at a time to find out more about the business and conditions of work.

- **Approach customers** and ask them as many questions as possible, including one important question: "Why do you choose this business over a competitor?" There is no single answer to this question. Every customer has a different response and reason for choosing one business over another. Which includes quality, location, customer service, price, speed, convenience, friendliness, etc. A few years ago, I was performing my due diligence for a business I wanted to purchase. In talking to a few customers I asked, "Why do you chose to bring your business here instead of to a competitor?" The answer was shocking. I received the same answer from most of the customers. "Because I had a bad experience at the other place and I will not go back." None of the answers were because I love this place. For me that was a sign of opportunity. Both businesses were taking customers for granted. If I can improve customers' experience, and exceed their expectations, I can increase profit exponentially.

- **Visit all competitors**, use their services, and compare. What are their advantages and disadvantages? What about their location, work process, bottlenecks, customer service, product quality and service? Observe and write everything down. Talk to employees and customers if possible. Are there too many competitors surrounding your proposed business? Are they competing on price instead of service?

- **Investigate Demographics**, visit city hall to research and review all demographics that are relevant to your type of business: population, age, ethnicity, gender, education, labor force, average income, unemployment, etc. Is development moving toward you or away from you? Are there plans for more competitors to open around you? Compare the trend of traffic, is it increasing or decreasing in front of your potential new business?

1. **Economic Action:** Write down your specific plan on how to remodel, landscape, improve quality, operational expense, speed of service, improve customer count, increase dollars per transaction, boost productivity, replace some employees, train existing employees, install new equipment, eliminate all bottlenecks, add *"Wow"* experience, atmosphere, offer unique value propositions, cut down expenses, etc.

2. **Strategic Action:** Create a Unique Value Proposition to set yourself apart from the competition and give customers many reasons why you should become their business of choice (as you will read in Chapter 5, "Can You See Me"). Create your strategic marketing plan using the four levers of how to increase profit exponentially (as discussed in Section V, The Strategic Principle).

3. **Tactical Action**: Create your sales training manual that is specific for the sales people, including PowerPoint presentations, brochures, business cards, and menus. Familiarize staff with all materials. Train sales people to improve their closing ratio and their dollar per transaction. (Covered in Section VI, The Tactical Principle).

4. **Test Action:** Survey customers' reactions, employees' feedback, sales results, and gross profit based on strategic and tactical actions you have taken. Then fine-tune operations. I recommend a private opening to test your operation first.

5. **Launch**: Be prepared for the grand opening and invest in marketing the grand opening day weeks before you open. The following are ideas of what to do at your grand opening:
   - Rent a billboard to drive customers in on the grand opening day for discounted or free products. This can include buy one get one free, a free gift card with every purchase or 50 percent off certain products.
   - Promote on radio and TV. Local TV ads are reasonably priced and many stations will create your ad for free.
   - Have a radio station on site for the event.
   - Hire a professional to write a press release about you, your managers, your grand opening, amazing offers, entertainment, and send it to all the media.
   - Print ads in your local newspapers about the grand opening specials.
   - Visit companies in your area and offer the management incentives to pass on your flyers to their staff and customers.
   - Rent a booth in any function going on such as fairground, home exhibit, car show, etc. Collect email contacts and give them irresistible offers or free widget if possible.
   - Once customers come in, make sure to offer some great incentives for them to spend more money that day and for them to come back.
   - Create a buzz on opening day with offering e.g. a free helicopter ride, a NASCAR on premises, a celebrity to meet for a picture opportunity.
   - *"Wow"* the customers with speed, quality, experience and friendly staff.

NOTE: All incentives, coupons and special offers should have an expiration date to create a sense of urgency.

"Success is by design not by accident."

CHAPTER 5

Can You See Me?

Every business should have a Unique Selling Proposition (USP). USP is a marketing concept that was first proposed in the 1940s by Ross Reeves. I personally prefer to call it Unique Value Proposition (UVP) because most clients hate to be sold but like to have added value in every purchase. The purpose of a UVP is to solve a problem and give customers reasons to switch to your brand even though you are in a commodity business. An effective UVP must be one that the competition either cannot, or does not offer. It must be unique and desired by customers. The proposition may be lower price, better value, convenience, free coffee, higher quality, friendlier service, speed, guarantee, etc. When the concept was first introduced, UVPs were very effective, but modern customers have become savvier and understand that not every catchy slogan is true. Therefore, new UVPs need to have a guarantee to be believable and effective.

Unique Value Proposition

How to come up with your UVP?

- Put yourself in your customers' shoes. Too often we fall in love with our services and forget that it is the customer's opinion, not ours, that matters most.
- Step back, talk to your customers, and listen to their complaints and satisfactions about your business in general.
- What do they like most or least about your business or industry?
- Sure, customers come in to buy your products or services, but is that all what they want?
- Why don't they purchase from your business more often?
- Do they also buy from your competitors every now and then?
- What makes them come back and drive by the competitors to come to you?

- The real reasons customers buy from you may be surprising. The answer might be quality, atmosphere, convenience, speed, friendliness, neatness, guarantee, customer service, or price.
- Price is never the main reason people buy. Even if your competitor has a lower price, your customers definitely have reasons to still patronize your business.
- Ask your customers what they like least and most about your industry, and build your UVP around their answers to solve a problem while creating a niche.

Hall of fame UVPs

- "The King of Pop"
  — Michael Jackson

- "The Greatest Show on Earth"
  — Barnum and Bailey Circus

- "It's the Real Thing"
  — Coca-Cola

- "Think Different"
  — Apple

- "Just Do It"
  — Nike

- "Diamonds Are Forever"
  — DeBeers
- "The Ultimate Driving Machine"
  — BMW

- "We Deliver"
  — Domino's Pizza

- "The World on Time"
  — FedEx

These are great UVPs. Each of them helped to make the respective company or people, leaders in their field. However, the following two UVPs stand out as the main reasons behind the success of their respective companies.

FedEx

- "When your package absolutely, positively has to be there overnight."

FedEx's slogan was clear, positive, different, and new. It was what many businesses and consumers needed. No one before had ever offered a guarantee like this. It solved a problem.

Domino's Pizza

- "You get fresh, hot pizza delivered to your door in 30 minutes or less or it's free."

Domino's slogan is a prime example of a great UVP. It filled a void and solved a problem and complaint. Not only does it guarantee a fresh pizza delivered to your door in 30 minutes or less, but if it's not delivered within 30 minutes, it's free. It is really a complete statement that solved a big problem at the time it was prepared. It would sometimes take an hour for a pizza to be delivered by other pizza companies, and by that time it was no longer fresh and hot. Domino's recognized the issue and built their niche around it. The "free" was icing on the cake. Consumers were ordering Domino's and clocking the time, hoping to get their pizzas for free.

There are several questions to ask about your business to determine a UVP:

1. What are the unique services and values you offer that set you apart from your competitors?
2. What are the unique services, values, and experiences customers love to have?
3. What are the most common complaints customers have about your line of business in general?
4. What differentiates your business from the competition?
5. What are the main complaints customers have about your competitors?
6. Can you solve the above problems?
7. Why do customers go without your product or service even if they need it?
8. Which of the above factors are most important to the customers?
9. How do customers feel after using your services?

10. What kind of experience do customers have while visiting your premises?
11. Which of the above factors do competitors not easily imitate?

You should construct your memorable UVP out of these unique, meaningful qualities. Communicate your UVP to your customers via all your print and media ads and monument signage. Remember, a UVP doesn't mean anything unless it's backed up with a guarantee. Take care of your customers' concerns and your customers will take care of you.

> *"Give your clients so much value so they think you are crazy!"*

SECTION III

THE WIN-WIN

PRINCIPLE

CHAPTER 6

I Don't Like Your Business

Socrates

In the fifth century BC, a great philosopher in Greece came up with the conclusion that Socrates was the wisest person in Athens. When Socrates heard the news he had his doubts and decided to investigate for himself. He went around Athens talking to all philosophers. Later Socrates came to the same conclusion, that indeed he was the smartest person in Athens. When asked how he came up with that conclusion, he replied, "All philosophers I talked to believe that they know everything. Me, I know that I don't know, therefore I ask questions."

The goal of being in business is to make money for services you provide to your clients.

Therefore, you must ask yourselves the following questions and find the solutions to secure your success in winning the daily battles and to ultimately win the war.

#1 — What are the main customer complaints in my business and industry?

#2 — What are my main challenges as a business owner in my company and industry?

Customers' Main Complaints

With more than two decades of business experience, and after talking to many customers and doing a lot of research and reading, I have concluded that the five main complaints customers have in the carwash industry apply to many other industries:

1. **It takes too long.** Almost all customers hate waiting in long lines. Many people will go to the restaurant that doesn't have the long wait. Just like

people at a store will try to get into the shortest line possible. The biggest complaint people have at a restaurant is after ordering their food: it takes a long time to be served. People hate to wait!

2. **The employees aren't helpful or friendly.** Customers go to businesses expecting to deal with knowledgeable and friendly employees. When employees are not educated about the business or have not bought into your business culture and mission statement, the customers judge the business as a whole. Many customers will not return to the business if they had a bad experience with employees.

3. **The business is not attractive.** You've heard the saying "image is everything." That applies to the exterior of your business as well as the landscape. Is the overall exterior of your business appealing? Does it give the image that you run a professional business? And do customers feel confident to do business with you?

4. **Poor quality of product and service.** Consumers want high quality products or services rendered. If I have my car washed, I expect a clean car. If I eat at a restaurant, I expect good tasting food. If I don't like the quality of your service or product, I might not come back.

5. **It's too expensive.** Or I don't see the value in what I paid. It's rarely about the price—it's about the perceived value. Customers only complain about the price when they have problems with one of the above issues. What am I getting back for my hard earned money?

> *"Your price advantage can be easily duplicated, but a strong customer service culture is difficult to copy."*

Providing good service does not make customers loyal to your business. Customers expect, at the very least, good service. Your business might be conveniently located for them, but they may go to one of your competitors in between the time they visit yours. It doesn't take much to make them convert to one of your competitors, unless you provide great service that your competitors cannot match.

Customers don't care about you, they believe in the following: WIIFM or What's in it for me? Until they know how much you care about them, it's all about them. They do not buy your product or service; they buy what the product or service does for them. They are buying the great feeling of ownership, happiness, and the experience.

Business owners should strive to commit to the following:

- Commit to excellence in every aspect of the business.
- Demand excellence from all employees.
- Commit to a great customer experience.
- Empower all employees to provide a great customer experience.
- Create an employee focus group to develop breakthrough customer experience.
- Make it easy for customers to do business with you.

> *"Help your clients fulfill their dreams and watch your business soar!"*

CHAPTER 7

Stop Nagging

Ben Franklin said, "Beware of little expenses. A small leak will sink a great ship." Those words are so true today.

It doesn't matter what your gross income per month is if your expenses are 101 percent of your income or more. Business owners look at this economic downturn as a recession, and their priority has become cutting down labor and controlling expenses.

Typically, the biggest expense of any business is payroll. In some service businesses with an extensive labor force that is poorly managed, their payroll expenses may be up to 60 percent, although many businesses fall between 20-40 percent. Many business owners automatically reduce their labor force or cut down labor hours when they are short on money and need to increase bottom line profit. This short-term solution may cause long term ramifications, including customer dissatisfaction and decreases in business volume and cash flow. When a business has to lay off employees without proper planning, everyone loses—customers, employees and business owners.

Controlling labor and expenses should have been a priority from the first day after opening your business. Especially in good times. If 10 percent extra in labor expenses is equivalent to $6,000 per month or $72,000 per year, or $720,000 in ten years, and if you include taxes, workers' comp, and compound interest, that's over $1,000,000. (These numbers are based on $60,000/month labor costs.)

Cutting back on labor without a properly implemented plan is really counter-productive since it creates more customer complaints. That is called a win-lose situation—a win for your competitor and a loss for you. Unfortunately, any business that is labor intensive cannot eliminate its labor force.

In a carwash business, for example, the main reason customers skip washing their vehicle is that the carwash process takes too long. So how does a business improve operating and productivity processes, and cut down labor expense, while maintaining or improving customer satisfaction? It is essential for a business to study its operating efficiencies, time-motion studies, floor plan configurations, bottlenecks, and management policies, among other things. If it normally takes forty minutes to wash a car and you cut down the wash process time to twenty minutes, isn't that already a 50 percent savings in labor costs? Once the business has increased productivity and improved the time it takes to perform tasks, the owners can then reduce the labor force.

Employers' Challenges

The five main challenges facing employers are:

1) Labor cost per customer is too high

This is a very important point. Employers should break down all their expenses to cost per customer or transaction. Another good practice is to divide yearly expenses by the number of days they are open for business per year, then divide the answer by the number of hours doors are open for business. It's a good measuring system to control all expenses on an hourly basis. That way employers know how much income they need to make per day, or per hour to be more precise, to first break even and then to make money. Sam Walton famously used this technique when he founded Wal-Mart, currently the world's largest retail chain store with over ten thousand stores worldwide and two million employees. He used a simple method to figure out how much income each store needed on a daily basis to break-even and start making money.

Sam Walton took the average monthly expense of each store including labor, supplies, and all variable expenses, and then divided the total by thirty. He shared that information with the store managers and pushed them to promote and sell to reach that dollar number as early as possible every day because all income after that point was pure profit.

What lessons can you learn from Walmart?

- Treat all of your expenses as fixed expenses.

- Learn at what point during the day your business breaks even and you start making profit.
- Let us assume that your daily break-even point is $2,000 and you're open ten hours a day. That breaks down to having to make $200 per hour. Armed with this information you have two choices:
  - Reduce the time it takes to reach your daily break-even point by pushing the sales, offering ridiculous incentives to customers such as early bird specials, buy one get one free, 50 percent off "x" amount of products, etc.
  - Offer the above incentives at the top of every hour to secure your $200 break-even point. Or if your goal is to achieve at least 30 percent profit, set your hourly goal for $300 in sales per hour. Share the information with your managers and sales team.

2) Labor productivity is low

How do you calculate labor productivity? It's the number of customers or the number of paid tickets per hour divided by the number of total employees working during the same hour. What is labor productivity? It's the measurement of how efficient your work force and operating process is. For example, if you have ten customers per hour and you have ten employees working, then your labor productivity is one. If you have twenty customers per hour and ten employees, then your labor productivity is two. To be profitable, the productivity rate should be figured on per man-hour spent. Each business can have a different profitable productivity rate depending on their industry. Labor productivity is in direct proportion to how efficient transactions/tasks can be accomplished. The question all operators should be asking here is, "How can we become more efficient?"

3) Customer count is low

Like any business, if we do not have a certain number of transactions per day, we cannot break even. Increasing customer count is not an accident. Though increasing the number of leads or customers is sometimes a hard or long process, it is the blood of our business. Holding onto existing customers is essential in increasing the customer counts. You don't want to concentrate on attracting new clients while existing ones are leaving.

4) Sales dollar per transaction is low

Many owners try to lower their prices to draw more customers. What they don't realize is that lowering the price may increase volume, but not necessarily the bottom line. Lowering the price may result in more expenses, i.e. power, labor and payroll taxes and even worse, customer complaints. Lowering prices is a quick fix that may cost more in the long run. Most businesses work on a small margin of profit. Therefore, lowering prices is not always the right answer as long as your price is very competitive with the market.

5) Labor percentage from total revenue is high

When labor percentage of the total income is high, it is a sign of trouble. However, labor percentage may be deceiving and may be lower or higher than what the indicators are showing. If you have many accounts receivable, or if you sell a good deal of gift certificates, gift cards, or prepaid services where jobs will be performed on a later day, that can manipulate labor percentage. Using the wrong metric could lead to higher labor dollar expense, or to customer dissatisfaction and loss of business. I recommend watching the following indicators in combination with the overall labor percent to have a better grasp of your business: productivity metric, as well as the labor dollar per transaction, and sales dollar per transaction.

CHAPTER 8

Light Bulb

To resolve the issues facing customers and operators, it is helpful to compare and contrast their concerns.

Look first at the similarities.

Create Win-Win Solutions

1. It takes too long

Customers skip using your service because they know it takes too long. How does this common customer complaint affect a business' bottom line? Because it takes too long, many customers will skip using your service because of time constraint.

This is a major complaint among customers. As stated in a previous chapter, customers hate waiting. Bottlenecks hinder many business systems, limiting the number of customers served per hour. Managers must identify their business' bottlenecks and solve these problems in order to speed up their processes and increase overall customer satisfaction. Methods to solve time problems can be anything from investing in more productive equipment, improving staff productivity, eliminating bottlenecks, reviewing and questioning company policies as they may be the cause of the delays, and hiring better trained staff, if needed.

Resolving this major complaint would improve the business bottom line. It would also help solve the following problems for the business owner.

- Customer count is low.
- Sales dollar per transaction is low.
- Labor costs per customer are too high.
- Labor productivity is too low.
- Labor percentage per sale is high.

> *"The popular phrase, 'Time is money' is wrong. Time is more than money – it's gold. The present time is priceless"*

Here are some approaches you can use to increase efficiency in your business.

Equipment

From my experience in the carwash business, employers can save up to 50 percent of labor cost by installing the proper equipment and changing from hand carwash to machine-wash. What about in your business? What equipment can you add to eliminate labor, improve speed, productivity, quality and/or customer experience? This can be anything from a better and more efficient database register, to a prep machine, or the proper monkey wrench. Proper equipment can eliminate bottlenecks, saving time, labor, and money. Even in bad times, if upfront cost is a concern, many banks or companies will provide 100 percent financing for new equipment.

Assembly line

Inspired by meat packers, Henry Ford innovated the moving assembly line that spurred the new industrial revolution in factories around the world. Because of the assembly line techniques, Henry Ford reduced the time it took to assemble the Model T car from one car every twelve and a half *hours* to one car every twenty-four *seconds* and reduced the price from $850 to $300. By the time the Model T was discontinued in 1927, more than fifteen million Model T cars had been sold, accounting for nearly half the automobiles in the world at that time. On an assembly line, employees have to perform their duties in a set time by work process or by conveyor speed. Can you turn your work process into an assembly line?

Teamwork

Retrain employees to improve productivity using the 80-20 Pareto principle, which was created by an Italian economist that proved 20 percent of something is responsible for 80 percent of the results. Change the workforce from individual to teamwork. Why should one person do all the work while other employees stand around not helping? Furthermore, why don't employees working in one department help people in other departments that could use the help? Do employees get paid from their department or from the company as a whole? Teamwork is more effective than individual effort.

This is how the Pareto principle works. If 20 percent of the employees are doing 80 percent of the work, then it should be easy for managers to identify the 20 percent star employees who should be role models and the standard all employees should follow. Team up one of your star employees with another employee. Have each employee work on the same task together. This forces your slower employee to pick up the pace and finish at the same time as your star employee. Your star employee will force the other employee to work harder and faster. Therefore productivity will increase. If 1+1=2, in business 1+1= 11. If a task normally takes one person 10 minutes to accomplish, as a team of two with proper training, the same task may take only 3 or 4 minutes.

Japanese versus automakers in North America
Companies who invest in training and teamwork have more employee involvement, better quality work, better customer service, more profitability, more productive employees, and better efficiency. A study was done comparing American and Japanese automakers in North America. It was determined that the American automakers spent forty-six hours training employees. Furthermore, less than twenty percent of the time employees worked in teams. As for the Japanese automakers, they spent three hundred seventy hours training employees. However, more than 70 percent of the time employees worked in teams. In conclusion, it cost the Japanese automaker 16 percent less time to produce a vehicle and with 21 percent less defects. In the end, training and teamwork is more advantageous and is crucial for business success.

Database system
A database system (DBS) is a must in any business. It can speed the transaction process. A DBS is a great tool to help learn customers' names, provide personal service, help track purchasing habits, and provide an automatic specific coupon or recommendation to customers per their buying habits. A DBS controls prepaid cards, loyalty programs, and automatic recharge of membership programs. All of these features may speed up the transaction process. Furthermore, managers today must have

a DBS installed to track by-the-minute sales price per customers, customers per man-hour (productivity), employees' costs per customer (labor cost per customer), and overall labor percentage. The DBS companies incorporate state-of-the-art dashboards that cut through the noise and essentially give a radar view of your business. Dashboards can also gaze into the future and show potential pitfalls in business. Sophisticated dashboards also incorporate the concept of what-if-analysis. For instance, one can simulate the business impact of increasing the sales dollar per customer, simply by moving a dial on the dashboard.

> *"Time is free, but it's priceless. You can't own it, but you can use it. You can't keep it, but you can spend it. Once you've lost it you can never get it back."*

2. Employees are not friendly

Why do customers view your employees as unfriendly? Who is responsible? Where does the buck stop? Are employees loyal to the business? Have they been properly trained? What effect does it have on the bottom line?

What if an employer builds a culture of being the servant of his/her staff, as discussed in chapter three? What if employees were very motivated and loyal to the business, properly trained, and had clear mission and vision statements that customers are the most important person in the business and customers are the boss that we need to please? What if this belief was reinforced every day? How would that affect the business and would it help solve the following problems?

- Customer count is low.
- Sales dollar per transaction is low.
- Labor cost per customer is too high.
- Labor productivity is too low.
- Labor percentage per sale is high.

> *"Take care of your clients' problems
> and yours are solved"*

3. The business is not attractive

Suppose you are driving down the street and you start having car problems. You need to stop immediately to have it checked. Luckily, you are at an intersection with two mechanics' garages. The first one looks great, it is well-maintained, nicely landscaped, freshly painted with nice earth-tone colors, has blacktop asphalt, looks well kept, is clean, and has a professional monument sign. The second mechanic's building needs a new paint job, looks dirty and neglected with an old monument sign, and overall the place looks run-down.

Which one would you trust with your vehicle? Which one gives you the sense of trust and professionalism that makes you feel more comfortable taking your vehicle to? Keeping your facility well maintained helps bring more customers to your business. It gives customers a sense of trust and projects an image of success. Customers like to patronize successful businesses, and receive great experiences in return.

Having a well-maintained facility may help solve the following concerns of the business owner:

- Customer count
- Sales dollar per transaction is low
- Labor percentage
- Gross income at the end of the day
- Labor costs per customer

> *"Image is everything!"*

4. Product/service and quality are poor

What if you visited a local restaurant for the first time and the food quality was bad? What if the service was bad? Would you give it a second chance? Would you recommend the restaurant to your family and friends? If not, then would you blame your customers for not coming back and not recommending their friends? How many clients have problems with your facility and leave without saying anything and never come back? For every customer that complains, there are many who left without saying a word. Every complaint should be considered a red flag and handled immediately to prevent it from reoccurring in the future.

Poor product quality has a direct effect on:

- Customer count
- Sales dollar per transaction low
- Labor percentage
- Gross income at the end of the day
- Labor costs per customer

5. It's too expensive

Most customers will feel that your prices are too high only when they have a complaint about one of the above four reasons. It's never about how much it cost; it's about the value. If it's about the money, then everyone will be driving a Tata Nano, the world's cheapest car that costs $2,500. Some of you may drive expensive cars that cost $100,000 and never complain about the price. Did you get a good deal (value) for what you paid? If you purchased a $100,000 car and made a deal to buy it for $90,000, then you got a great value regardless of the cost. You will brag about it to all your friends and family. What if a dealer lists the Tata Nano at $5,000, is that a good value? No, why not? It is an $85,000 savings compared to the $90,000 car. Most likely you will not purchase the Tata Nano because:

- It is priced too high for what it's worth.
- It's not about how much you paid—it's about the value.
- It does not have the most desired features and benefits— safety, style, comfort, power, image, and status —you want most in a car.

Let me ask you a question. What is your favorite restaurant? What kind of ethnic food do they serve? When you decide to go out to eat, how many other restaurants do you drive past to get to your favorite place? How many restaurants do you pass that provide the same authentic food as your favorite restaurant? Why do you prefer to go to that specific restaurant? Is it because of the price? Of course not. Then what is it? Is it the atmosphere? Experience? Quality of food? Quantity of food? Friendly service?

> *"It's never about the price; it's always about the value!"*

The Price Is a Perspective

A point of view. Let's say you are walking down the street and you see a pen in a store window and decide to buy it. From your first look at it, you put a $20 value on the pen. You then walk into the store and ask about the price. To your surprise, the salesman tells you it costs $100. What would you do? I assume you'd say, "Thank you." and turn around to walk out. But then the salesman says, "Hold on a second." He gets the pen and hands it to you. He also hands you a piece of paper and asks you to start writing. He says, "Notice how smooth the pen writes; notice how it's so comfortable to hold between your fingers. This pen is made from a rare material. This is the pen that Queen Elizabeth keeps in her purse. This is the same pen the President of United States uses to sign bills into law. The pen is valued at $250, but the manufacturer decided to lower the price for a limited time because he believes every person deserves to own one of these rare pens."

Is the pen still worth $20 in your mind or did the value go up? Did the value of the pen in your mind change from $20 to $100? Are you willing to pay more for the pen now that you know the real value of the pen? What if the salesman tells you there is a sale today and you can have the pen for $75? What would you do? Wouldn't you purchase it? You went from $20 to $75—that's over 300 percent more than you wanted to pay. What changed your mind?

Knowledge of the history and quality of the pen helped build a value. Therefore, you were willing to pay more. It's not how much you pay that's important, but how much you get back for what you paid. Once you make the price your main marketing tool, it's all about how cheap you can get it, regardless how good your is service and quality.

In conclusion, price is never an issue to customers unless they have a complaint about something else. When customers complain about the price, what effect does it have on the business?

- Lower customer count
- Sales dollar per transaction is low
- Lower sales price per customer
- Higher labor costs per customer
- Higher labor percentage

CHAPTER **9**

Let Them Complain

Complaints Are Opportunities

As a business owner, many things beyond your control may affect your business. You cannot control a slowdown in the economy or the number of competitors around you. But customer service is 100 percent within your control. Business these days is fiercely competitive; therefore, no business can afford to lose a customer. Although most companies know they can't afford to lose business, many companies don't take consumer complaints seriously. Exceeding a complaining customer's expectations is a strategic principle of any business.

I've been to many businesses, and while I am talking to the owner, a customer approaches with a complaint and asks for the manager. To my surprise, some owners deny that they are the owners and point to the manager to handle the issue.

The most loyal customers in any business are those who had a bad experience that was solved in a manner that exceeded their expectations. These customers become the best word of mouth advertisers and promoters of the business. Customers who have their complaints brushed off or not taken seriously still use word of the mouth to talk about the business. However, it is a lot of negative things about the business. Not listening to and adressing a customer complaint can be one of the most harmful things to the business, as this customer will tell whoever will listen, horrible things about you (even if many of the things aren't true).

A few years back before the Internet and social media, an upset customer would spread the word of his experience to people close to him. Today their opinion and thoughts can reach hundreds or thousands of people in a

85

matter of minutes. Ultimately, it is up to us as business owners to decide what kind of word of mouth and reputation we want to have from those customers.

> "Solve your clients complaints and your problems will be solved!"

You Are in Control of Your Client's Blog

I cannot control the customers' blog and social media, can I?

The answer is, yes you can! There is no such thing as chance or luck. Everything happens according to the law of cause and effect. The law of cause and effect states that our actions dictate what the re-action would be. You are in control of your actions and the reaction is a direct result of how you handled the problem. That is what Buddhists call *Karma* and what the Bible preaches as, *You reap what you sow.*

Let's say a customer approaches a manager with a complaint, such as a product was broken when they opened the package. Managers, as emotional human beings, immediately take a defensive position to protect the business and declare that the product was not broken at the time of purchase and the customer must have done something to break it. This causes the customer to leave upset and mad. The end result—the manager wins the battle but the business loses the war.

Every great structure begins as a blueprint, and then a strong foundation is built to sustain the structure. Same with every great business, it started with a blueprint and a step-by-step plan to ensure the success of the business. A step-by-step checklist on how to turn a complaint into an opportunity with a win-win solution for everyone involved is an essential part to running a successful business.

Before I give you a checklist on how to turn a complaining customer to a most loyal customer and a spokesperson of your business, here are some facts.

Fundamental Rules

- Customers aren't always right, but they always have to leave winners.
- 98 percent of all customers are honest.
- Would I want to punish 98 percent of my customers because 2 percent are dishonest?
- If the customer truly believes the damage happened at the business, regardless of whether it did or not, then the truth doesn't matter at this point.
- Customers are always right, even when they are wrong.
- Customers are our bosses. We all need to keep our bosses happy or we will be fired.
- We are dependent on our customers for business survival.
- If customers leave upset, then our competitors win. I refuse to have my competitors win.
- We cannot fire customers, but customers can fire us by choosing to go somewhere else.
- Customers must leave happy so they come back.
- Keep the end goal in mind. What is the end resolution we would like to achieve? (You want the customer to leave happy and come back).
- Every time a customer leaves upset, we cannot force them to come back.
- Take care of the customer, make sure they leave happy so they will come back.
- I want the outcome to be a loyal customer who will leave positive feedback online.
- An upset customer will leave negative feedback online and damage our business reputation.
- Keep the emotions out of the equation and do what is in the best interest of the company (a happy customer).
- If you doubt that the damage happened at the business, please do not argue with the customer. Keep your opinion to yourself.
- If the customer honestly believes the damage happened at the business, please do not argue with the customer to prove him or her wrong.
- Your job is to be the consumer's advocate.
- We speak one hundred to one hundred fifty words per minute, yet we can listen up to four hundred words per minute. Therefore, a customer has an ample amount of time to form an opinion about us based on our body language and tone of voice. Though we judge ourselves by our intentions, others judge us by our behavior. Be aware of your body language and tone of voice as you are speaking to customers.

> *"Your best clients were customers*
> *with complaints!"*

Four Different Outcomes

For resolving an issue with a client, there are four different outcomes:

- **Lose-Lose**: where both parties lose.
- **Win-lose**: The customer wins and the business loses the argument.
- **Lose-win**: The customer loses and the business wins the argument.
- **Win-win**: This is what we are seeking to accomplish. Win-win takes more energy and creativity to achieve than the other three. Win-Win doesn't mean that you give in to what the customer wants (that's called win-lose) or the customer giving in to your wishes (that is called lose-win), but it means you find a better solution that both can agree on. Better than compromise, synergize. Synergy is the working together of two things to produce a result greater than the sum of their individual effects. The origin of the word synergy comes from the Greek word synergia or synergos, which means, "working together." I recommend reading the book, *7 Habits of Highly Effective People,* written by Steven Covey, which covers this subject in detail.

Three different Types of Customers

- **Repeat Customers**: These visit your business at least once every three months. They are the top 20 percent of your customers who bring in 80 percent of your revenue. Calculate the lifetime value of your customers to realize how much these customers are worth to you. Let us assume that the average repeat customer spends $100 per month or $1,200 per year. Those customers stay with you for an average of ten years. That is equal to $120,000. Knowing the lifetime value of those clients, can you afford to lose them because of a small complaint or damaged product?
- **Regular Customers**: Those who visit your business once or twice a year still have a lifetime value. Calculate it.
- **First-time Customers**: Will they become one of the 20 percent or 80 percent group? Who knows? The real question is, can you really afford to lose any of them?

Not all customers are equal and one solution does not fit all. At the same time, you want to always come up with a win-win solution because you can't afford to have a bad reputation. You always want to keep those repeat customers who are part of the 20 percent that are responsible for 80 percent of your income at any cost. What about regular and first time customers? Are they really less important customers? Are they the daughters, sons or spouses of repeat customers? Did existing customers refer them to you?

Because each business is different, I will cover how to handle an alleged damage on a customer's car after the wash. I would suggest:

- If damage did indeed happen at the business, you should have procedures in place on how to handle the incident.
- If the damage the customer claimed is easily repaired by your detailers, e.g. a light scratch, a scuffmark, or a sticky gummy substance that looks like a scratch, then assure the customer that you will fix it for them. First explain why it did not happen at the carwash and how the wash process is safe; then clean it or buff it out at no charge and maybe even give them a free wash for next time.
- If the damage is minimal such as broken side view mirror that you can purchase and install for less than $100, consider if would you want to lose a customer and all his family and friends and get bad reviews online for such a small amount?
- Make a deal with a near-by body shop that has a detail account with you and they will repair your damaged cars at wholesale prices. Basically, this is a trade business. In this case, your cost becomes very minimal.

Turn Complaints into Opportunities

- If you track customers by purchases, then run a report to find out the frequency of visits.
- Approach with concern and sympathy.
- Apologize for whatever happened.
- Introduce yourself, tell them your name and ask for their name.
- Call them by name.
- Assure the customer that you will take care of the issue.
- Assure the customer that you want to make sure they leave happy, and you want to earn their future business.
- Have the customer complete an information form, with their name, address, phone number, email address, and incident information. The information form is a very important step of the process. Note: Do not call the form a complaint form.
- Ask the customer if they would like anything to drink as they are filling out the form.

- Listen to the customer without any interruption.
- Feed the information you just heard back to the customer and have them elaborate more.
- Ask questions to clarify the story.
- Ask if they saw it happen? Did other customers see it happen? If yes, then excuse yourself to go talk to those witnesses before going any further. If no witnesses, go to the next step.
- Examine the car for other damages near the alleged damage and all around the car.
- Ask if the customer was aware of the other damages.
- Conclude if any of the existing damages caused the alleged damage. Do not discuss your findings with the customer at this time.
- Wait for the customer to tell his/her side of the story and answer all the questions then say, "I listened to your side of the story, now may I tell you my side of the story?"
- Tell the customer, "First let me assure you that I appreciate your business and want you to keep coming back. I will do whatever it takes to make sure you leave here happy."
- "I have been "x" years in business and from my experience this could not have happened at the carwash and here are the reasons why."
- "The mark on the car is red and we have no red color polls or walls."
- "You see the damage here next to the alleged damaged? This is the reason and the cause of the alleged damage."
- "The scratches you are claiming are circular and our machines wash the car in a horizontal direction. Walk with me, let me show you the equipment." (Turn around and walk without looking back, the customer will follow). If customer refuses to follow then explain to them what you were going to show them.
- "Please put yourself in my shoes; we have hundreds of customers that come in everyday and many times customers try to claim damages on us when it is not our fault. I'm not saying you are trying to do this."
- "You see those three disclaimer signs we have, they all say that we cannot be responsible for damages."
- "I believe that you are honest and you truly believe that this happened over here. Am I right? And that is why I want to make sure I take care of you and keep you as a happy customer."

  "I hope you understand my position. From my experience the damage costs about "x" dollars to repair. Our policy is we do not pay cash for any damage that we don't believe we are responsible for. I can give you credit for the same amount to keep you happy."...Or exceed the customer's expectation and offer 150 percent credit.

90

Note: If the customer seems very, very upset, and out of control when you first approach them, the best way to handle it, is by putting yourself in their shoes and feel what they are feeling and let them know that by saying:

- "I know how you feel. If I were in your shoes I would feel the same way." Or
- "I know how you feel. It is very frustrating to come in for a carwash and leave with damage."

Then follow up with the above step-by-step checklist.

If acknowledging customer's frustration technique does not work and customer is out of control, then the manager should take the information form from the customer and assure them that the owner will call them to take care of the issue. Use this alternative method to avoid a major conflict at the business and for the customer to calm down before you try to synergize and come up with a win-win solution.

> "Clients aren't always right, but they always have to leave winners!"

SECTION IV
THE SYSTEM PRINCIPLE

CHAPTER 10

The Biggest Business Expense

To help you gain the unfair advantage, I need to challenge your beliefs on what is considered assets, what is considered expenses, and what is the real cost of providing a customer with a product or service. Therefore, I need to start by asking some questions that will help you break out of the box and change your perspective on how to calculate the above three items.

What Is the Biggest Expense in Your Business?

Take a minute to think before you give your answer. The obvious answer is not always the right answer. I encourage you to start thinking out of the box. One of my favorite quotes is "The level of thinking that got you where you are today, will not take you where you want to go." The answer may shock you.

To give you a hint, the answer is none of the following:

- It is not your mortgage or rent payment.
- It is neither the interest payment nor the cost of your equipment.
- It is not your fixed expenses.
- It is not the water and power bills.

Then what is it? Could it be labor expense?

Most people, when asked the same question, rush to answer by saying payroll. If you think the biggest expense is labor, then you are wrong. As a matter of fact, you are not alone. I typed the same question on Google search looking for answers. The most common answers were payroll, insurance, advertising, cost of goods sold, inventory, bookkeeping, and the list goes on.

We are conditioned to think the way we do, mainly because of tax codes and our friendly Certified Public Accountant.

Did you know that per tax codes, excess inventory is considered an asset not a liability? And because of the tax code and our friendly Certified Public Accountant, we are conditioned to believe the same. Yet surplus inventory ties up business working capital and should be considered a liability. If a company received a big order and used up inventory that has been sitting in their warehouse for a long time thus freeing up their working capital, per tax code, that is considered a loss of assets. In reality the big order received, freed their cash capital and made them a lot of money.

Going back to the question at hand. The biggest expense in a business is the time when:

- No customers are being served.
- Employees are getting paid waiting around for customers to come in.
- Equipment is idle because of lack of business.
- The register is not doing Cha Ching.

> *"Whenever you have no production and money is not coming in, then your expenses become infinite!"*

No production equals a missed revenue opportunity. Serving more clients every hour of the day can make or break a company. Unfortunately, most businesses are leaving tens of thousands of dollars in revenue on the table each and every year because of the lack of understanding of this simple principle. If you are only open for business a few hours a day, you must make every minute a productive minute. Every time employees are standing around waiting for customers, is a lost revenue opportunity.

I have the same challenge at my carwash. When we wash fifty to sixty cars an hour, our lot looks empty and my staff stands around about twenty-five minutes per hour waiting for cars.

Increasing the number of new customers, increasing sales dollar per purchase, and increasing the frequency of visits of existing customers are the three approaches for more revenue opportunities.

I've been to many carwashes on the weekend where they were packed and they couldn't fit one more car through the wash per hour. Many customers washing their cars that day think that the owner is making a killing because of the packed lot. Looks are deceiving. Many of these carwashes look so busy because of the bottlenecks in their operations. Many of them don't wash more than twenty to twenty-five cars per hour. Are you aware of the bottlenecks of your business?

In reality, measuring the throughput of the carwash (or any business) is the fastest way to evaluate if a business is profitable. Measure success of a carwash by how many cars are leaving the lot every minute, not by how many cars are on the lot. Those packed carwashes were taking forty-five minutes to an hour to wash each full-service vehicle because of the bottleneck in their operation.

The number one reason people skip going to service oriented businesses is because of time constraints. Time is not money; time is more valuable than money. In fact, time is gold. You can always acquire more money, but you can never acquire more time. Everyone has the same twenty-four hours of time in a day. While you can never have more than twenty-four hours in a day, you can certainly choose how you allocate the time you do have. You can easily save an hour or more per day by eliminating the tasks and activities that are not urgent or important. If your service takes too much time from a customer's day, then stop wondering why your customer count has dropped and start thinking about what are you going to do about it.

In the past, I was guilty of the same. I have since learned how to eliminate all bottlenecks and increase throughput with a more efficient system in order to gain the unfair advantage over the competitors.

"Take care of the minutes and the hours will take care of themselves!"

CHAPTER 11

Diamond in the Rough

Although the next question is easy and simple, and everyone whom I've asked knew the answer, it is an essential question to glue the big picture together. I will use another example from the carwash industry.

- Assume a well-managed carwash washes twenty cars an hour
- With an average of $20 per transaction, for a total gross income per hour of $400.
- Labor expense is 40 percent
- Fixed expense is 20 percent
- All other expenses total 20 percent
- Net profit is 20 percent

After deducting all expenses the net profit is $80 per hour. What if the owner ran some promotions and was able to drive in five extra cars an hour. The question is, what would the cost be to wash these five extra cars per hour?

Cars washed per hour	20
Dollar per car	$20
Gross sales per hour	**$400**
Labor Expense -40 percent	-$160
Fixed expenses -20 percent	-$80
Other expenses -20 percent	-$80
Net Profit	**$80**

Double your profit in one easy step.

Because the carwash is well managed, that means the carwash has no bottleneck issues, leaving employees enough time to wash those five extra cars without the need to add one more person to the clock. Therefore, all the expenses and labor cost remain the same, except for the extra cost of water, power and chemical to wash those five extra cars, which is about $1 per vehicle or $5 total for all five vehicles. If the average ticket per transaction is $20 that means the net profit from those five extra transactions is 95 percent or $95. The carwash owner has doubled his net profit just by washing five extra cars an hour.

Cars washed per hour	25
Dollar per car	$20
Gross sales per hour	**$500**
Labor Expense	-$160
Fixed expenses	-$80
Other expenses	-$80
Cost for washing 5 extra cars	-$5
Net Profit	**$175**

If your business involves selling a product, then deduct the cost of products from the extra income and the balance is your net profit. If you are in the restaurant business, what is the cost of serving five extra customers per hour? Isn't it just the cost of the food? Using this formula what is your cost of serving five extra clients a day? Can you see the new opportunities? Can you promote and sell to new businesses or clients below your previously calculated break-even point and make your competitors wonder how you can sell below your cost and stay in business? The problem business owners often focus on is the cost of working instead of focusing on the cost of not working. For example, if a restaurant during regular business hours normally has five vacant tables, and through promotions is able to occupy two of those tables with hungry clients, this add-on has a direct effect of increasing the net profit by about 100 percent as explained above.

Should Labor Be Considered a Payroll Expense?

Business people are conditioned to see payroll as labor expense because, per the tax codes, that is the way the Certified Public Accountant reports it. My question to you, should your entire payroll be considered as labor expense? Let me ask the question in a different manner. Can you open your company's doors for business without any labor involvement?

If the answer is no, then what is the number of employees you need to have at any given moment when you are open for business? It depends on what type of business you have; it could be two, six, or any number. Assume that you need a minimum of five employees whenever you are open for business. Your labor cost is $10 per worker that amounts to $50 per hour or $500 per day labor cost just to open your doors for business, regardless of whether you are bringing in business or not.

I urge you to challenge the assumptions you were given by your Certified Public Accountant and tax laws. If this expense is mandatory every time you open the company's doors for business, why not consider this portion of labor cost as an hourly or daily fixed expense? Better yet, if your average monthly labor cost is $30,000, then why not look at this number as part of the fixed expense? That means your daily labor cost is $1,000 and your hourly labor cost is $100. That means that your hourly fixed expense includes $100 for labor cost. That is a simpler way to calculate your hourly expenses.

On the same token, there is an easier way to calculate if you are making money on an hourly basis. Take your total yearly expenses, including labor and cost of goods sold, and divide that number by the average number of days you are open for business per year; then divide it again by the number of hours you are open per day. Doing so will shift your way of thinking and gives you a better picture of how much money you should generate per hour or per day to break even before you start making money.

What Is Your Bottom Line Cost?

I will use another example from the carwash industry. Using traditional thinking and assumptions, let us assume that the normal charge for a complete detail is $200. The complete detail includes clay, buff, wax and interior steam clean and it takes the three detailers about three hours to complete. Therefore at $10 per hour per detailer, the total labor cost for a complete detail runs you $90 and about $10 for other expenses for a total of $100. If the customer negotiates the detail cost and offers to pay $100 for the complete detail, you will never approve it because per traditional thinking $100 is the break-even point.

> *"Focus on the cost of not working rather than the cost of working!"*

Good operators and innovators may ask themselves the following questions to tackle this issue:

How can we reduce detail labor cost?

- Are there any new training techniques that we can teach the detailers to speed up the work process, therefore cut down labor cost?
- Is there any new equipment that can help speed up the detail process and lower labor cost?

Great operators and advanced innovators, will challenge the assumptions of the profitability by using the theory of limitations (TOL). Along with the above questions asked by good operators, the great operator asks the following out-of-the-box questions:

- Is the true cost of my complete detail one hundred dollars?
- How can I do a complete detail for one hundred dollars and still have a big margin of profit?
- How can I reduce my detail cost down to almost zero?
- At what time of the day, or under what situations, can my complete detail cost be zero?

Understanding the first two questions of this chapter makes it easier to understand and realize how detail cost can become zero under certain circumstances. If your total operating cost, including labor, remains constant when washing five extra cars per hour, then the real price for washing these five extra cars is the additional cost of water, power and chemicals. The same applies if you detail a car. If you can manage to detail a car without adding extra labor, then the real cost is only the extra charge for water, power and chemicals. For all practical matters, your profit from that detail is one hundred percent!

> *"The biggest cost is the cost of not working during which interest has to be paid while equipment does not earn!"*
> *Peter Drucker*

Because the purpose of owning a business is to make money, every measurement we use in the business has to satisfy one question: "Does it help make money?"

To satisfy the above question, there are three, and only three simple measurements a business has to adopt and implement. The measurements are: Throughput, inventory, and operational expense. The definition of each measurement has to satisfy the question, "Does it help make money?"

Throughput is the measurement of money coming into the system. It is the rate at which the company generates money through sales of finished products or services. Throughput is the only method by which a company makes money. It is measured by the number of finished products or services rendered by a company per year, month, day, week or hour.

Inventory is the measurement of money currently inside the system. It is defined by the amount of money the company has to invest in buying goods that it intends to sell to generate money. If you are in the retail business, your inventory is all the products that are on your shelves (or in a warehouse), that you intend to sell to generate money and cash flow. If you are in the restaurant business, your inventory is the raw food in your refrigerator that is used to create the final product—the delicious meals your customers ordered.

Excess inventory ties up business working capital and should be considered a liability, on the other hand lack, of inventory will affect the throughput and the profitability of the business.

Service businesses, with no inventory, such as carwashes, are calculated differently. The number of cars that are waiting in line to be attended to, vacuumed, washed, and cleaned are considered inventory. The only limit to how many cars a carwash can process per hour is measured by the speed and length of the conveyor. If the throughput of the conveyor is one hundred cars per hour, and one hundred cars per hour are driving in for a wash, yet only fifty cars per hour are being washed and cleaned, then the excess car inventory of fifty cars per hour is lost opportunity because of existing bottlenecks in the system that are costing the business hundreds of dollars per hour. We can look at it the opposite way as well. If only fifty cars are driving in for a wash every hour and the carwash can process one hundred cars per hour, then the lost opportunity is due to lack of inventory. The throughput is affected and the business loses hundreds of dollars per hour.

Operational expense is the measurement of money a company has to invest in order to turn inventory into throughput. Most businesses invest in advertising and promotion to bring customers to their business. That is also part of operational expense. As discussed previously, operational expenses are composed of all yearly fixed and variable expenses including labor, mortgage, utilities, (excluding cost of inventory), divided by the number of days you are open for business, then divided by the number of hours you are open per day. Knowing your hourly operational expense is a vital piece of information to be a profitable business.

CHAPTER 12

What Type Are You?

Productivity Versus Budget Versus Result Oriented

Owners need to focus on whether to train their managers to be productivity oriented, budget oriented, or result oriented. The following examples show the difference between the three and some of the problems that can arise.

A company has a three million dollar budget for its three departments. Each department gets a one million dollar budget and the department's budget is managed independently.

Department One's manager is very efficient and uses the 7 Mindset Principles. He weighs the success and profitability of his department by promptly addressing any system limitations. He measures productivity and throughput. He also keeps a good watch on inventory and operational expenses. As a result, he accomplished the goal of his department with half the allotted budget and saved $500,000. Therefore, on the books it seems that his department was over-budgeted by $500,000.

Department Two's manager wanted to make sure that his superiors did not come back to him at the end of the year, questioning his management skills because he deviated from the budget. Therefore he made the budget his priority. At the end of the year he felt he accomplished his mission and did a good job because his department's expenses were equal to the projected budget.

Department Three's manager was result oriented. He did not care about productivity or the budget as long he could reach the results expected from his department at the end of year. His priority was to achieve the results expected from his department, no matter what the cost. The result was his department spending 1.5 million dollars, going over the budget by half a million dollars.

Because Department One was under budget and Department Three was over budget, the company took the $500,000 saved from Department One and reallocated it to Department Three's budget. Because of the reallocation of money, the total budget for all three departments still balanced at three million dollars. The owner is happy.

The following year, because of the slow economy, the company needed to cut every department's spending by 10 percent. With this cut, which department gets hurt the most? Which department will complain the most? What will most likely be the end result for the company? The most likely result for the coming year with this spending cut is all three departments will not meet their goals.

Department One gets hurt the most because they already had high productivity and throughput the previous year and can't cut anymore without affecting the business. Department One will not meet their goal because the previous year they came in under budget by eliminating all bottlenecks and excess operational expenses. With this budget cut they cannot eliminate any more.

Department Two just met the budget the previous year and will most likely have some hard time meeting the budget again.

Department Three will complain the most because dollar wise they had the biggest cut. The only reason they have the biggest cut is because they went over budget the previous year and an additional $500,000 was reallocated to them. Most likely Department Three will, again, be over budget.

As you can see from the previous example, although managers need to understand the importance of productivity, budgets and results, managers should strive to master the operation principle. To help managers think and work this way, what incentives can you, as the owner, offer the department to improve productivity, cut expenses, speed up the process, become more profitable, increase customer satisfaction, etc.? How can you ensure that managers won't spend excess cash, or the surplus, on meaningless things so they come in on budget instead of under budget?

You should have future budgets determined by measuring productivity. Not by looking at last year's budget to determine the next year's budget.

Many companies offer incentive programs for managers who come in under budget. Great incentives for these managers give the manager a percentage of the excess cash as a bonus. For example, if you offer 10 percent of the surplus as a bonus and the manager's department comes in $100,000 under budget, the manager would receive a $10,000 bonus. This type of incentive ensures that the manager won't spend the excess cash just to come in on budget. And he will save the company a lot of money, which affects the bottom line by increasing profit.

It should be noted that incentives should only be offered when the products or services are still of high quality and no corners were cut.

There is always a solution for every challenge. In this example the company should move Department One's manager to Department Three and move Department Three's manager to Department One. Department One's manager, because of his efficient management system, will most likely save about 50 percent of Department Three's budget. Department Three's Manager should be held accountable to keep and enforce the system that is already in place in Department One.

> *"In the emerging real time business environment, speed and agility area are a decisive advantage."*

Good Business Practice

To be continually successful in business, one must meet the demand. Although this might seem obvious and simple, it can be quite tricky. At a glance, it may seem good to have long waits for your business because it means you have so much business coming in that you can't keep up with the demand. Although it may appear that your business is doing well, this is counter-productive to building a long-term successful business. It is possible that these long waits will last for a while but soon the customers will get tired of this situation and disappear.

The long wait may give the misconception that you are making a lot of money and gives other entrepreneurs the opportunity to open up similar operations in your area. People hate to wait! If another store, which sells the same products or services as yours opens up across the street, many customers will go there because it doesn't have the long wait. This will take part of your business because you couldn't keep up with demand.

Demand for Harley-Davidson motorcycles was so great that the company was unable to keep up with customers' orders. That gave opportunity for other motorcycle companies, such as Honda, to enter the business.

To prevent others from entering your market you must meet demand, control operational expenses and inventory, and eliminate bottlenecks and system limitations. By doing so, you keep your fixed and variable expenses much lower than the competition. You may choose to sell your widget at a lower retail price than your competitors. Your competitors may think you are crazy and that you are losing money. In reality you will be driving them out of business.

In order to keep up with demand, you must:

Understand the demand. To do this you should take a step back and objectively analyze your business. How many customers come in on different days? Different times of the day? And different times of the year?

Make sure not to overstock or under stock your products. This relates to the first point of understanding the demand. You don't want to overstock products that can't be sold within a reasonable time period. Overstocked inventory ties up business working capital and becomes a liability. Yet you don't want to under-stock products to the point that they sell out and affect your throughput and cash flow.

Know how many workers you must have to meet demand. Although you don't want to have extra workers standing around with nothing to do, it can be just as bad to not have enough staff on hand for busy periods. Understand your demand and staff as needed. It is better to have extra staff than to be short and affect your productivity.

Train your employees well and hire good workers. Your employees must be trained to perform well under pressure and to work as teams to increase productivity. Although they first need to be trained well, they must also be good workers that will buy into your culture.

Invest in necessary equipment. If equipment can increase throughput, lower inventory and operational expenses, then it is imperative to invest in new equipment.
Review your operation policies. Very often company policies and procedures may be the cause of delays and customers complaints.

Employees' Wants and Needs

Humans love attention (good or bad), which is why employees should get recognition for good performance. A big problem many businesses face is workers acting negatively in order to get attention. This type of behavior is natural for most people because we were raised that way! From the time we were babies, we have gotten attention when we acted negatively. Although the attention we received wasn't necessarily good attention, i.e. we were being punished or yelled at, we learned how to get noticed even if through bad attention. This is known as a positive re-enforcement for negative behavior (such as getting bad attention from a boss). This type of behavior can be very detrimental for a company, as some workers may do things, which could hurt the company's reputation or success.

One way to stop this behavior is to build the culture we discussed previously. You catch people doing good things and recognize them for it—and enforce the teamwork policy.

> *"Every morning in Africa a gazelle wakes up, it knows it must outrun the fastest lion or it will be killed. Every morning in Africa, a lion wakes up. It knows it must run faster than the slowest gazelle, or it will starve. It doesn't matter whether you are the lion or a gazelle; when the sun comes up, you'd better be running."*
> *Christopher McDougall*

CHAPTER 13

Theory of Limitations

Eliyahu Goldratt, a physicist, was the first person to optimize production techniques by explaining how to identify the bottlenecks and the thinking process to eliminate the system constrains. In 1986 Goldratt published his findings as a fictional story in his book, *The Goal.*

Performance of any company is dictated by its limitations. Bottlenecks prevent an organization from maximizing its performance. Theory of Limitation (TOL) is applied to measure company performance from two different perspectives.

Is your system performing at its best?
Does the system lack resources to reach its best potential?
Below are some bullet points to give you an idea about Theory of Limitation:

- It helps identify the bottlenecks in a business and provides a step-by-step thinking process to remove the limitations. It applies the technique of cause and effect to tackle the issue at hand.

- A limitation is anything that prevents a system from achieving its highest performance possible.

- If a system can produce more, then more should be produced; otherwise, there is a limitation that should be addressed.

- If a company has downtime for lack of demand, that is a limitation.

- Limitation may be caused from supply shortage. This might be the number of customers per hour who come into a business or shortage of parts for an assembly line to complete a product.

- Limitation may be caused by management policies.

- Limitation may be caused by a system in place that cannot keep up with demand.

There are five steps to identify the constraints. But first, write down the goals of the company for the existing operation.

- How many orders do you want to deliver per day?

- What is your goal for your labor dollar per customer?

- What is your labor percentage goal?

- What is your goal on how much time it should take to process each order?

- What is your break-even point?

The Five Steps for the Theory of Limitations

1. Identify
2. Control
3. Prioritize
4. Analyze
5. Repeat

Step One: **Identify the limitation**. What is your weakest link? What part of the process is a bottleneck and slowing down your overall operation? The weakest link can be easily measured by timing each process or by simply watching your employees or your equipment throughput and the excess number of inventory waiting to be processed. If each procedure takes one minute to accomplish, except for procedure "X" that takes five minutes, then that may be your bottleneck.

Step Two: **Control the limitation.** After you identify the limitation, investigate the cause of the bottleneck and correct it. A bottleneck may be caused by: lack of employee training, lack of productivity, lack of capacity, or lack of staff. Just keep in mind that the cause of the limitation may not be tangible. It may be intangible—such as: company rules and policies or lack of training and productivity.

Step Three: **Prioritize the limitation.** The identified bottleneck should have priority over every step in the process. Increasing the throughput of the bottleneck will increase the overall throughput of the system.

Step Four: **Analyze the system limitation.** Review how the system is working after you have corrected the limitation. Evaluate if the correction solved the bottleneck issue or just improved it. If the identified procedure is still causing a system limitation, repeat steps two and three, such as, invest in new equipment, hire more staff, re-train all personnel, etc.

Step Five: **Repeat the process to identify a new limitation**. Systems can only have one limitation at a time. Once the identified limitation is removed, repeat the process to identify and solve a new bottleneck.

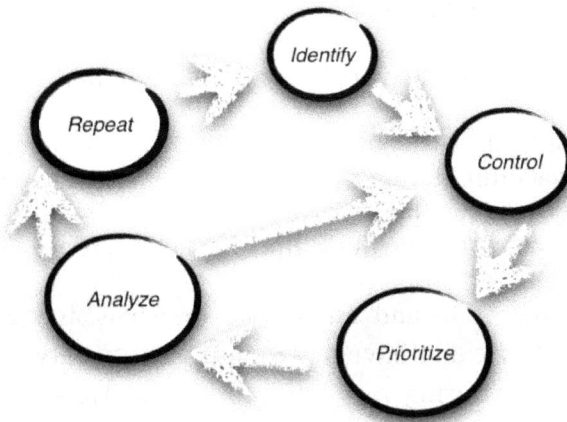

Measure Your System's Performance

The limitation might sometimes be seen by the naked eye and not need any measurements. At other times you may need to time each process from start to end. We will again use a carwash as an example and measure the individual time of each process.

> Customer's wait time to get their wash **ticket**: 2 minutes.
> Time to **vacuum**: 4 minutes.
> Time waiting in **loading** area to enter the wash conveyor: 2 minutes.
> Time to **prep** on the conveyor before the wash: 2 minutes.
> Time in the wash **conveyor** tunnel: 2 minutes.
> Time to clean the car at the **finish** line: 6 minutes.
> Time for customer to get in their car and **exit** the wash: 2 minutes.
> **Total** throughput time: 20 minutes.

Ticket	Vacuum	Loading	Prep	Conveyor	Finish	Exit	Total
2	4	2	2	2	6	2	20

Identify the LIMITATION

Now that we know the definitions of the Theory of Limitation, let's put it into practice.

From looking at the chart above we can see two limitations: the vacuum takes four minutes, and the finish area takes six minutes.

With visual inspection of the work process we find that:

The vacuum is not a bottleneck, although each car takes four minutes. There are two vacuum stations; therefore, every two minutes one car is ready and taken to the loading area.
Visual inspection confirms the finish line as the limitation.

Note: Twenty minutes in and out of a carwash is adequate time. Most carwashes wish they could have a throughput of twenty minutes per car. The challenge comes during very busy hours. The time it takes to wash a car could be delayed because if the parking at the finish line is full of cars, then the whole operation is affected. The conveyor has to be stopped. All processes up line are affected and create their own bottlenecks. The total time to wash a car will increase dramatically and may easily double.

Per the Theory of Limitation, we identify only one bottleneck at a time. Therefore, the limitation is at the finish line. Once the limitation is identified, control it by investigating to determine the cause. The root of the problem may be tangible or intangible.

Intangible causes may be company policies, work procedures, lack of motivated or trained employees Maybe low grade chemicals being used in tunnel are cleaning cars poorly so that staff is spending extra time cleaning manually.

Tangible causes may be that employees must re-clean wheels manually because of lack of adequate equipment in the tunnel to produce a clean wash. Or wheel-cleaning equipment may not be installed in the tunnel, and staff must clean wheels manually. Maybe staff is taking their time on cars, doing extra work to get extra tips, or one person is assigned per car instead of two, or a shortage of employees, or no manager on site to motivate and speed up the cleaning process.

It may take time to eliminate the cause of the limitation in the finish line cleaning area. Repairing or investing and installing new equipment cannot be done quickly. Therefore, prioritize the limitation over all work processes. Because your throughput is only as fast as your slowest task, a temporary quick solution may be to relocate some employees to the finish area from other departments, hire new staff, slow down the conveyor speed, or maybe change the sequence of the system by moving the vacuum step to the finish area and combining both processes and both labor forces. Once you correct the problem, analyze the changes to make sure that the limitation has been removed, otherwise, keep on working on the issue until the limitation is removed. Finally repeat the process, check for new limitations in the system.

Note, many times when a limitation is removed a new one is born.

Once you repeat the five steps to identify a new limitation, you may determine that the prep time is a bottleneck. Once the prep time is replaced by a piece of equipment, the prep time becomes zero. When the prep limitation is removed, the loading time will automatically disappear too. The loading time existed only because of the prep bottleneck. Loading cars on the conveyor and sending cars through the wash shouldn't take any time. Looking at the chart above the vacuum becomes the new limitation. The solution would be to either add more vacuums or relocate the vacuum procedure to the finish area.

Before you decide to invest in new equipment ask yourself the following questions:

- Would this new piece of equipment help make more money by increasing throughput? If productivity doesn't increase, the new piece of equipment is an unnecessary expense.
- Would this new piece of equipment increase throughput while simultaneously reducing both inventory and operational expense?
- If you take advantage of all the features and benefits the new piece of equipment offers what is the return on investment? Please note that return on investment could be tangible or intangible.

"A chain is as strong as its weakest link."

SECTION V

THE STRATEGIC PRINCIPLE

CHAPTER 14

Four Levers to Increase Profit

Forget about going out looking for customers. Forget about pushing customers to invest in your product or service. When you push, you are pushing customers away from you. Instead, stand out and become the lighthouse that everyone is dependent on. The question is what can you do strategically to gain the unfair advantage and to attract more customers? How can you stand above the competition and become a magnet that draws customers to you without you having to search for them. You will find the answer in the implementation of the four levers.

There are four effective levers, and only four levers, to increase your business

Increase Customer Base	Increase Sales $ Per Purchase	Increase Frequency of Visits	Control Operational Expenses

1.Increase customer base.

2. Increase sales dollar per purchase.

3. Increase frequency of visits.

4. Control Operational expenses.

The great Pyramid of Khufu in Egypt is one of the few remaining wonders from the Seven Wonders of the Ancient World. Khufu's Pyramid is built entirely of limestone. This pyramid, which is considered an architectural masterpiece, contains around 1,300,000 blocks ranging in weight from two and a half tons to fifteen tons and covering thirteen acres. Ancient Egyptians were able to move obelisks weighing more than one hundred tons. Did you ever consider how ancient Egyptians were able to accomplish unparalleled human feats that are not even possible with today's advanced technology?

The simple answer is that they relied on brain more than brawn. Archimedes is considered, along with Newton, to be one of the founders of mathematical physics. As one of the great mathematicians of all times, he combined a genius for mathematics with a physical insight. Archimedes provides us with the answer to the burning question above.

> *"Give me a place to stand, and I shall move the earth with a lever."*

Archimedes, who lived in the third century, understood the power of levers and formally penned their correct mathematical principle. The word lever comes from the French word *lever*, which means to lift. You can think of the four effective levers mentioned above as four levers that enable you to apply a small force in order to raise a very heavy object. The heavy object in question is the net profit.

Test the Levers

Let us take the four levers to increase business and apply them to a service business.

- Assume XYZ company serves 5,000 customers per month.
- The average customer spends $25 per transaction.
- Their frequency of visit is once a month.
- Total Revenue is equal to $125,000.
- Total operational expense of this business is 80 percent of revenue or $100,000.

Total operational expenses is devised from

- Labor expense which is calculated as 40 percent of revenue or $50,000,
- Cost associated with providing the service is $1.25 per customer which is equal to 5 percent of purchase price or $6,250

- All other expenses—fixed expenses, insurance, rent, promotion—35 percent or $43,750

Customer Base		Sales $ per Purchase		Frequency of Visits	=	Revenue	-	Total Expenses 80 percent	=	Net Profit 20 percent
5,000	x	$25	x	1	=	$125,000	-	$100,000	=	$25,000

As you can see, the owner of this business has a net profit of $25,000. It is hard to increase net profit by 10 percent, but as we know, a journey of 1,000 miles begins with a single step. The same principle is used here. Don't worry about increasing the net profit; instead let's concentrate on increasing each of the above income levers by 10 percent.

> *"There are two kinds of people; the first kind believes it is possible but very hard, and the second believes it is hard but very possible."*

Each income lever increased by 10 percent

Customer Base		Sales $ Per Purchase		Frequency of Visits	=	Revenue	-	Total Operational Expense	=	Net Profit
5,500	x	27.5	x	1.1	=	$166,375	-	$108,075	=	$58,300
10 percent increase		10 percent increase		10 percent increase		33 percent increase		65 percent decrease		133 percent increase

Observe the following:

- Increasing monthly customer count by 500 and increasing frequency of visit by 10 percent or 550 extra return visits per month should not increase labor cost. The 1,050 extra customers per month breaks down to 35 extra customers per day or 3.5 extra customers per hour for a 10-hour workday. A business that handles 167 customers per day, or 17 customers per hour can most likely handle extra 3.5 extra customers per hour without the need to add an extra staff member.
- Labor dollar remained the same at $50,000 but labor percentage of total operating cost is now at 30 percent instead of 50 percent.
- The dollar cost of total operational expense is higher but the total percentage of operating expense is lower.
- The only extra expense incurred is the cost associated with providing the service, which is 5 percent of purchase price or $2075. What if we had to add an extra staff and labor increase by $6,000? Therefore total operational expenses increases by $8,075.
- As I mentioned previously, systemizing work process, eliminating bottlenecks, and installing the proper equipment can cut down labor costs even with additional customers. Controlling operational cost and increasing productivity is essential. It is the key for a business to grow exponentially.
- Notice revenue increases by 33 percent not 30 percent that is called exponential increase.
- Finally, look at the net profit. It has increased profit exponentially from $25,000 to $58,300. That is a 133 percent increase.
- Increasing sales dollar per car by 10 percent and frequency of visits should be very easy to accomplish, as will be discussed later.

Take a moment and think of your own business. How would a 133 percent increase in profit benefit your business or your personal life? If you could increase your total profit by 133 percent, how many dollars does that translate to every month? Calculate the answer and then realize that this is how much you are losing every month. The question is how much are you willing to invest to get such results? Your investment is not necessarily money—it could be investment in time and research.

The money is in your parking lot. You just have to know how to get it. The fastest way to increase the revenue of any business is by improving the closing ratio and increasing the sales dollar per transaction. I have personally cut the closing ratio of many companies by 50 percent and increased the sales dollar per transaction by up to 100 percent within thirty days. If you improved your higher package offer by adding a lot of value and incentives, would it become a no brainer for prospects to invest in the higher end package? What if you add a risk-free money back guarantee to make it easier for the client to invest in better-packaged service or product? What if you improved your marketing approach, received proper training in sales, and were able to increase customer base and frequency of visits by 10 percent, and increase the dollar per transaction by 30 percent, what would the result be?

The results are in the following chart.

Customer Base	x	Sales $ per transaction	x	Frequency of Visits	=	Revenue	-	Total Operational Expense	=	Net Profit
5,500	x	32.5	x	1.1	=	$196,625	-	$109,589		$87,036
10 percent increase		30 percent increase		10 percent increase		57 percent increase		56 percent decrease		248 percent increase

As you can see, the total operational expense increases slightly because of the 5 percent cost associated with providing the service. Though the higher priced package was promoted, labor dollar remains the same because it is still the same amount of customers, therefore labor percentage dropped to 25 percent of the total revenue. You can see how revenue has increased to 57 percent and net profit grew exponentially to 248 percent. A 30 percent increase in sales dollar per customer and only 10 percent increase in customer base and frequency, amount to 248 percent increase in net profit. Take a moment to think of your own business. How much are you willing to invest in money, time, research, and out-of-the-box thinking to get such a result?

In the following section we will cover potential strategies for each of the above levers.

> *"Money is in your parking lot, you just have to learn how to get it."*

I - Increase Customer Base

This strategic information and the additional tools will help you gain the unfair advantage and increase your customer base.

Lifetime value

Increasing your customer base will dramatically grow your carwash profit exponentially. First you need to learn the lifetime value of each new customer you acquire who becomes a raving fan. Once you have that number, you will understand how important it is to actively work on automating this process.

Do you know the lifetime value (LTV) of your raving fan customer? Your raving fans are the top 20 percent of your customers who produce 80 percent of your income. LTV is perhaps the most significant and one of the most overlooked measurements in business. It gives you an idea of how much repeat business you may expect from each client and helps you determine how much you should invest to acquire those clients. Depending on your business, it might be worth it to acquire a customer at a break-even point, or maybe at a loss, knowing that you will tremendously benefit later.

To figure the LTV of an average customer you need to first find the answers for the following questions:

- What is the average dollar per transaction of your raving fan?
- How many repeat visits per month or year?
- On average how many years will these customers remain with your business?

Once you have these answers, plug them into the following formula:

(Dollar per transaction) x (Visits per month) x 12 months x (Average number of years)

As an example, if once you acquire a customer, they spend $50 per visit, visit twice a month and remain with you for ten years. Then their LTV would be:

$50 per visit x 2 visits a month x 12 months x 10 years = $12,000

In my opinion this is only half the story—if each new client is very happy with your services, you exceeded his/her expectations every step of the way, and you have a good referral system in place. Consequently, each of your clients refers a total of three more new clients, then the real value of every new client is $12,000 x 4 customers= $48,000 of additional income in ten years.

Now that you have calculated the LTV of your clients, how much are you willing to invest to acquire a new client? Would you give the first service for free? Would you double the commission of your sales persons for every new customer they acquire as long as they retain their existing clients?

Many businesses understand the value of LTV, such as:

- The gym industry. Many gym owners offer first month free because they know that once a new member joins, he will be a member for an average of three years. Many of them will acquire a family membership and encourage their friends to join as well.
- Martial Arts. Dojo martial arts schools, offer free beginner martial arts classes, with free uniforms, at local gyms or Parks and Recreation Centers in hopes that those participants will join the Dojo to continue lessons for higher belt levels.
- An air conditioning and heating technician offers his first service call for $20 to cover his gas expense in hopes of doing extra services and setting these new customers up on his regular quarterly maintenance program.
- A carwash may offer a free, unlimited wash pass with any purchase as long the customer commits to renewing it for at least two months.

Keep in touch with existing customers

What good is spending money to promote and advertise your business to new customers if you do not promote to your existing customers? Follow up after a sale, make sure they are happy, and answer any questions they may have. Reactivate past clients by keeping in touch with them as well. Tools to keep in touch with customers include, customer relation management software, email, phone calls, CRM, text messages, and social media, etc.

Database system

Database software (DBS) is a great tool for marketing to your existing customers by offering them incentives to increase the frequency of their visit, as well as to increase sales dollar per purchase. The DBS will help you track frequency of visits, buying habits, inactive customers, collect email address, collect phone numbers, collect mailing addresses, collect birthdays, sell gift cards, promote prepaid cards, offer loyalty promotions, auto renew your memberships, on demand labor and sales reports, tighter control over all, and paperless reports. The DBS is an essential part of doing business. It will enable you to implement many ideas to lure customers back more often and to spend more money per visit.

Joint venture

Joint venture is a partnership arrangement between two businesses in which both parties agree to pool their resources for the purpose of promoting each other's services.

To increase your customer base, ask yourself:

- Who else provides services for my customers?
- Where do your customers normally shop before they come to you?
- Where do your customers shop after they leave your premises?
- What nearby businesses complement your business, but are not competitors, that you can join venture with?
- When your business increases, your suppliers benefit as well. How can your suppliers help improve your revenue?
- What kind of promotions could you exchange with those businesses that will be mutually beneficial?
- Are they willing to email their customers to refer your business and offer a special incentive?
- Would they promote your business to their existing clients?
- Could you drive more customers to their business?
- Can you appeal to their customers to come straight to your business after visiting one of those businesses?

Customer retention

Track the clients who have not been in lately, and offer them incentives to entice them to come back. Generally, the most loyal customers are those who go to a business that exceeded their expectations after having had a problem. The sad thing is, most business owners avoid dealing with customers who have a problem. Although it may be tough to deal with a mad or dissatisfied customer, avoiding or dismissing the customer altogether is a huge mistake.

On average, every business loses 25 percent of its customers each year. A database system helps you keep track of all your customers and their business transactions. After a few months of inactivity, send those customers personal letters or emails to invite them back and offer them an irresistible incentive. This method is tremendously successful in my business—we send all customers who were inactive for the last three months a personal email with my name and cell phone number and a message that I am concerned about them because I haven't seen them in a while. Over 25 percent of the customers come back and take advantage of the offer within thirty days.

On a regular basis, after we send the emails, I receive calls or emails from them thanking me for my concern, and promising me that they will be back. Sometimes I receive a call or a message with the following, "I was never going to come back because of my last experience, but because you cared and contacted me, I'll give you another shot."

Another retention marketing program is the customer comment card box. Comment boxes provide a great opportunity for you to retain unhappy customers and exceed happy customers' expectations even more. You should always call customers who leave a comment and thank them personally for their feedback. Customers who left positive comments are usually thrilled to have the business owner call them since it shows a great personal touch not offered at other businesses. You might follow up with a thank you card and a discount coupon enclosed or a free offer as a "thank you for your business."

Unhappy customers, on the other hand, are usually in total shock to hear from the business owner. This shows that their complaint was taken seriously and not just discarded. When calling the unhappy customer, make sure to apologize, promise to take care of the problem and ask them to give the business another chance. To top it off, offer the unhappy customer a great incentive if they come back within a week.

I also recommend having a sign with your picture, name, cell phone number, and a message to customers, encouraging them to call you directly if they are unhappy for any reason, or if the manager was unable to solve the problem or exceed their expectations. This is something that almost no other business does and will surely set your business apart from the competition. Because of the sign, your managers will perform better in your absence just to make sure customers do not call you with any complaints. Would you prefer an unhappy customer leave and never come back, or would you prefer they call you and give you a chance to make it right, and earn them as a happy, loyal client?

Today we live in a digital world. Make sure your clients can reach you through your website as well.

It is easier to re-activate inactive customers than to acquire new ones. Customer retention is an essential part of increasing customer base and profit. A 5 percent increase in customer retention may increase profit between 25 and 125 percent.

> *"Luck is when preparation and opportunity meet."*

Personal referrals

I want you to think of a service or product you recently purchased, and were so pleased with that you had to tell at least one of your friends about it. This is an example of a referral. Business owners often say, "I can't get referrals. I serve hundreds of customers per day—I don't have time to talk to each customer." This type of attitude is a recipe for disaster because 80 percent of new business comes from referral. The correct question to ask is can you afford not to have a referral system in place? Can you personally ask ten a day for referrals? Can you systematize your referral program and offer incentives to your staff and to the client every time they refer a new client to you? Can you automate your referral system?

You must exceed customers' expectations so they brag about your business everywhere they go. Once you give them service that exceeds their expectations, they will tell all of their friends about you.

Customers will not buy your product before they "buy" you. This is half the battle. Once a happy customer recommends your services to friends, their friends will automatically trust you. At this point, it is not a question of whether or not they're going to use your services, but which package are they going to choose. The situation is different and much harder with non-referred customer because first they have to trust you and like you before they are willing to do business with you.

My gardener for over ten years was telling me that he has one house in Malibu that he landscapes and maintains on a weekly basis, and he wishes he could get all the neighbors' business. I told him to get permission from his client to use his name as a referral. His current client is a social proof to the neighbors that he provides a good service. I prepared two different letters for him to distribute to the houses around his client's home every week when he is there maintaining the yard.

The first letter is about who he is, and the address of the house he maintains. The letter asks them to pass by and see the landscape and talk to the homeowner if they wished. It also asks to give him the opportunity to serve them with nothing to lose, because he was offering the first month for free as a thank-you for giving him the opportunity, regardless of whether they wished to continue with him or not. The second letter was from me personally as a client of his for over ten years. The letter is about how happy I am with his service. Three months later I followed up with the gardener and he told me that he had stopped distributing the letters because he now has thirty homes in Malibu.

Other ideas for referrals include:
- If you are working at a client's house, put a sign in the front yard and keep it for the duration of the job.
- Deliver flyers to neighbors of your client, informing them about your services and the house you are working on.
- After the job is done, ask the homeowner to invite neighbors and friends for a demonstration and offer free snacks.
- Actively ask clients for at least four referrals after a job is done. Ask if you can call them and mention the client's name.

- After a job is done, ask for a recommendation letter (which you write and have them sign). Ask if you can show it to future clients and/or distribute it to the neighbors.
- Offer incentives to customers who refer new clients to you.
- Send a thank you card after a job is done.
- Follow up with phone calls after a job is done.
- Follow up with an email, also when a job is done.
- Send birthday and anniversary cards.
- Call and email past clients at least twice a year.
- Call orphan accounts. Orphan accounts are customers who were dropped off the radar by other sales reps or because a sales rep quit.
- Learn the itch cycle of your product. If average consumers replace your product every three years, keep in touch with them and call them a few months before the itch cycle.

> *"Carry out a random act of kindness, with no expectation of reward, safe in the knowledge that one day someone might do the same for you."*
>
> *Princess Dianne*

Multiple streams of income

Robert Allen, my dear friend and mentor, is the author of many New York Times best selling books including, *Nothing Down* and *Multiple Streams of Income*. Thanks to his book, the phrase "Multiple Streams of Income" became very notorious.

With increases in wages, raw material expenses and inflation, every industry has been forced to raise its prices. Unfortunately, this has hurt many small businesses, because they had to raise their prices more than the big businesses. Nowadays, people are eating at restaurants less often and going to the big name stores such as Walmart, Best Buy, Macy's, Costco, etc., in order to save money and for one-stop shopping. This is negatively affecting most small businesses volume and income. Adding multiple sources of income and specialty services or products can be a good business decision to retain existing clients, bring old ones back, and attract new clients. Add services that complement your existing services, what clients need in combination with your services, or that clients may need before or after they use your services. Keep in mind many of the services you may offer could be outsourced or subcontracted.

Ideas for multiple streams of income include:
- Delivery service for restaurants. Some people don't like to eat at the restaurant due to time constraints, but would use the take out or delivery service of many restaurants.
- Grocery stores could institute an in-store-shopper by which the customers call in or email the desired products and the grocery's workers collect the products; have them packaged and ready for pickup when the customers arrive.
- Martial arts masters can make deals with nearby schools and gyms to teach kids beginner Tae-Kwon-Do in hopes that they enjoy the program enough to join his studio and continue with advanced classes.
- A martial arts studio may start an after-school program, where they pick up kids from school for tutoring classes and follow up with martial arts sessions.
- Add an extra service that you may promote, but the work is subcontracted out, such as a carwash offering windshield replacement or paintless dent removal.
- Joint venture with other non-competing businesses where you promote each other's services or products for a percentage of the sale.
- Solar companies may add home insulation services for customers who decide not to install solar panels, as well as, attic fans to reduce utility bills.
- Promote your new sources of income on your monument sign, banners, social media, in-house, flyers, billboards, radio, TV, direct mail and wherever else is appropriate.

Support fundraising
It's like having hundreds of people working for you for free to promote your business. Fundraising is a great opportunity to get involved in the community and impact people's lives. Let's say you make a deal with the fundraising director at a high school with four thousand students and you offer them 20 to 50 percent of all proceeds raised. Now you have a potential four thousand students or parents, plus faculty and staff promoting your business for free.

Social Media

Here are some statistics for social media.

- Monthly active users on Facebook reach nearly 850 million.
- 488 million users regularly use Facebook mobile.
- Over 77 percent of business to customers' companies and 43 percent of business-to-business companies, acquired customers from Facebook.
- 50 percent of Twitter users are using the social network via mobile.
- In less than three years, social media sites became the most popular destination on the Web, replacing pornography for the first time in Internet history.
- Consumers no longer search for discounts and special offers, rather the promotions find them.
- Consumers are having the information pushed to them from free subscriptions.

Armed with all the above information business have to:

- Add social media, such as Facebook, Twitter, and YouTube to their conventional advertising methods.
- Integrate Facebook, Twitter, and YouTube with their websites.
- If necessary, hire an outside company to build your page. If you don't have social media pages, what are you waiting for?
- Add a *Buy Now* button to your website for immediate purchases.
- Promote all your social media pages on all print advertising as well as on your monument sign and receipts.
- Claim your review pages from all search engines and edit the information about your business; add pictures and update them regularly.
- Take advantage of review pages, such as Yelp. They have an option to offer a deal to your viewers at a discount and promote your business.
- Encourage customers to leave feedback on-line.

Advertising

Conventional advertising is still effective, though it is on the decline. Television and radio advertisements are more affordable than ever. Television and radio companies make money from the advertisers. Their problem is, certain minutes per show are earmarked for advertisers. If they can't fill those minutes with ads, then the minutes are wasted and cannot be recovered. Therefore, they may accept an offer to trade business, and use the trades as gifts, to either listeners or vendors. In certain cases you may be able to trade 100 percent of your ads. In other instances, they may agree to trade only 50 percent of the total purchase.

Fleet Account
Fleet accounts at discount prices can make up for the slow-down of the day or the season, and creates a steady flow of business. Would you rather have no customers coming in through the doors or would you rather have them come in at a discount?

Fleet Account Employees Saving Card
Why only offer the discount to the fleet accounts? Why not offer the same discount to the employees of those accounts? You can always use more business.

Discount Day or Early Bird Special:
Offer a discount day to lure in new customers and build loyalty from existing customers. One day a week or maybe two days (usually the lowest volume days), offer discounted prices on specific products during off peak hours. For example if mornings are your slow time then introduce *Early Bird Special.*

II - Increase Sale Dollar per Transaction

Increasing the dollar per transaction is the fastest way to increase income. People will buy more than what they normally do if you give them enough reasons and incentives to do so. Money is always in your parking lot — you can get more money from your existing customers.

Here are some ideas to help you increase dollar per transaction:

Business to Business
If you own a business-to-business company, isn't it in your best interest to have your customer's best interest in mind? What if you invest in educating your customers on how to market and up-sell, or to increase productivity? Wouldn't that, in return, increase your profit? Wouldn't that make your customer see you as the expert in the industry and the go-to-person for answers? Wouldn't that increase the value of your company in their eyes and leave the competition lost in the dust?

Say an entrepreneur has a widget to sell and he is very good at marketing and selling it. In one month, he visits one hundred stores and sells each store one hundred widgets, just by educating the storeowners on the need for his widget.

Thirty days later he visits the same stores, and to his shock the stores have sold zero widgets. Can he sell them any more widgets? Might the stores' owners be thinking they made a mistake investing in the entrepreneur's widgets?

What should the entrepreneur do now to save his business?

Isn't it in the entrepreneur's best interest to train the stores' owners and staff on how to market and sell these widgets, by educating the consumer on the need of the product?

> *"Successful people don't wait for opportunities to present themselves, they create them."*

A chemical company makes millions of dollars a year by selling chemicals to hundreds of carwashes. The more cars these carwashes wash and the higher-end packages they sell, the more chemicals they consume, and the more chemicals they have to buy. Therefore, the chemical company benefits more when all their carwash accounts are very prosperous.

Question: What can the chemical company do to gain the unfair advantage? Should the chemical company leave their success to chance? Because they have the resources, they should invest in acquiring the knowledge of sales and marketing so as to help their carwash clients. The chemical company should educate the carwash owners, on how to increase car count, how to recreate a simpler wash menu full of incentives to make it a no-brainer for customers to upgrade to the best package. The chemical company should help train the carwash sales staff or create training video on how to increase sales dollar per car and distribute it to all their accounts. Even better—promote a webinar or a live seminar to all their clients to cover the subject and much more such as customer service and operational procedures to speed up the process and to deliver the best wash possible. As a result, the participating carwashes may realize revenues increased of

20 percent or more. Because of the increase in profit, many of these owners may open additional carwashes. Wouldn't that be a direct benefit to the chemical company? It is the power of the mass. When each carwash that participated in the sales training increase their profit, the chemical company's profit increases by a hundred fold. One hundred thousand dollars investment from the part of the chemical company into helping their clients make more money may result in additional million dollars in revenue for the chemical company.

> *"For your business to prosper, help your clients' business prosper first."*

Package your offers

When you go to fast food restaurants or movie theaters, notice that they offer packages and promote by asking you what package you would like and if you want to supersize it. The same marketing techniques should be used at your business. Offer packages with increased perceived value. Start your presentation by offering the highest package first. The highest package should have the best value and should include an irresistible offer. The total price of all the items in the package should be much higher than the price of the package. For instance, the value of the items in the package may be $300 but the package price may be $99. As a last resort, you may offer everything you provide *á la carte*. Costco perfected this concept by offering their products in bundles. Buy big and save.

Change your prices

What is the perceived value of your product or service? In many instances, a customer may think your product is not good enough if your prices are too low. Perhaps if you are a consultant and you charge too low for your services, a client may feel you are not qualified enough. Therefore if you raise your prices you may have more interested clients in your services. On the other hand if you are selling a service or commodity you may need to lower your prices to have more customers enter your establishment. Or maybe you don't need to lower your prices—instead just add more value or guarantee. Remember it is your clients who dictate at what prices you should offer your services. The only way to determine the correct pricing is to test the market. The pricing of your offers has a big effect on making the higher priced item the best selling item.

Many consumer behavior psychologists have conducted experiments about customers' behavior at a movie theatre. The experiments endorse a good strategy to increase sales dollar per transaction. At the concession stand, the psychologists rearranged the price of popcorn and offered small popcorn for $3 and $7 for large popcorn. The result was that 85 percent of the customers chose the small popcorn. When interviewed, the customers said they did not see value in buying the large popcorn for $7 dollars. Subsequently, the psychologists added medium sized popcorn for the price of $6.50. This resulted in 85 percent of the customers choosing the large popcorn. When interviewed, the customers responded by saying that they saw value in buying the large popcorn for $7, only $.50 more than the medium priced popcorn.

Simple menu
Your menu, or offer, should be simple with few options. Do not complicate and confuse the menu with too many choices. Customers prefer simplicity. Many sales are lost when offers are too complicated for the customer to make a decision. The number of packages you offer should not exceed three or four. If your company has wide range of offers, to keep it simple you make a decision on behalf of the customer and pick three options to present to the client and have them choose one. Or just recommend the best and most popular option and give them the reasons why. What made the fast food restaurant In-N-Out Burger® famous? Besides having fresh and quality food, it is the simplicity of their menu. Keep it simple.

Re-train ticket writers to become professional advisors
Sales is a profession, just like attorneys or doctors. The only difference is that attorneys and doctors have to spend a decade of their lives studying to earn their title and become the authority in their prospective fields. On the other hand, anybody could wake up in the morning and decide to become a salesperson. That's what gave the selling profession a bad reputation. But it doesn't have to be that way. With the proper training, sales people can become professional advisers and be considered as the authority in their field, rather than just order takers or ticket writers. Start a weekly training program. Make sure to offer your salespeople an incentive to sell more. Giving them incentives to sell is an essential part of your success. The

incentives should be incremental, depending on the dollars per transaction or on total revenue generated in a certain period.

Never make price the main issue

It is not about the price, it is about what the service or product can do for the customer. Obviously, customers will not pay more if salespeople make price the main issue. Part of the problem with unprofessional salespeople is that they put themselves in the customers' shoes too often. If they can't afford it, they assume customers can't afford it. So they promote less expensive products and make the price the main issue in their minds, which becomes a self-fulfilling prophecy.

> *"It's never about the price, it's about the value. It's not about how much I paid, it's about what do I get back for what I paid."*

Stop selling and start educating

Oftentimes customers may call or come in to your office shopping for the best price, either way do not discuss the price. If the customer calls on the phone, ask them to come in. Explain to them that you have many options with different prices. It is best if they come in so you can show them all the available options; explain the differences, advantages, and benefits so they can make up their mind which option is best for them. When customers are present, educate them on all the options, the processes, and the reasons why it is done that way. The more education and explanations you give them, the more professional they perceive you are, and the more they will consider you as the authority in the field and therefore more likely they will trust you with the job. When customers come to my carwash, for example, we educate them on the cause of the problem and the process to restore the car's finish. We may buff a sample on their car.

Signs or brochures

I can't tell you how many businesses I've been to that do not have any signs posted or handout brochures regarding their higher-end packages. It's like they're trying to keep it a secret. Post signs to promote and let customers know what you offer.

Samples and demonstrations

If possible, offer samples of the product or service. While customers don't always trust what you say, they trust their sight, taste, touch, smell, and hearing. With a sample, they will see the quality of the product or service. Costco has become famous for offering samples of the products they sell. Many customers will buy a product they previously knew nothing about, (many times they didn't even know the product existed), just because of a small sample. Many people have become lifetime customers because of a sample. It is a human behavior, when someone does you a favor you feel that you owe him or her back. Same when you give your client a free sample they feel obligated to purchase from you. That is called reciprocity.

Collect testimonials

Ask every satisfied customer to write a letter or record a short video complimenting your business. Make sure to post these for other customers to see. Carry these testimonials with you to show potential new clients. These letters will work as a third party recommendation. They may also work as a closing technique. If the client has a concern or an objection that is covered in a letter, you can say, "I understand your concern, as a matter of fact we had a customer who had the same concern in the past, but still they decided to go ahead with the service. They were so happy with their decision, they wrote us a letter about their experience. As a matter of fact, here is the letter, if you don't mind please read this paragraph."

When you ask your satisfied clients for a testimonial, many times customers will say they will write a testimonial, but they rarely do so. You should consider writing the testimonial letter on their behalf and take it back to them to sign it.

Risk reversal

The number one reason customers hesitate to make a commitment to invest their money is the risk of not getting their money's value. Promote your service with the following risk reversal guarantee, "If you are not happy for any reason with the product or service, you may replace the product or have the service re-done, with no questions asked. If you are still not happy, then your money will be refunded, no questions asked." When you offer a risk reversal guarantee that provides value and benefit, customers will appreciate your product or service more. The guarantee will force everyone in your company to raise their standards. The guarantee will also increase sales exponentially, by closing more sales at higher prices. When I offer the guarantee to clients, I follow up by saying, "Our philosophy is, if we don't provide you with everything we promised, we don't deserve to get paid. You work hard for your money and deserve to get what you paid for." This statement by itself closes the transaction for us. We have some customers who still want to shop around. We ask them to ask those competitors if they offer the risk reversal (which none do). After awhile they come back and say, "Your prices are higher than the competitors but I decided to bring you my business because I trust your services better."

Many magazines normally offer the first month for free, and you won't be billed for 30 days. Costco Wholesale offers one of the best guarantees. You may return any product any time for a full refund, no receipt necessary, (electronic items within 90 days) without the original box, even if you used most of the product.

How many companies do you know that offer risk reversal? What is better than your risk free, money back guarantee offer?

III - Increase Frequency of Visits

During a prospering economy, increasing the sales dollar per transaction is the easiest and fastest way for a business to grow their profit exponentially. The Great Recession has affected all businesses across America and the world. Consumers' income decreased and their spending habits changed. Many consumers still shop, but they are doing it less frequently and are spending fewer dollars per visit. It is easier to keep existing customers coming back than it is to find new customers.

In tough times like these, building and promoting loyalty programs and membership plans to increase the frequency of visits of customers has never been more vital for businesses to prosper. To encourage customers to become loyal to you and to increase their frequency of visits, you have to give them much greater value than you ever did in the past. A database system is critical for the automation of all your loyalty programs. Since all customers are not created equal, not everyone should get the same offer. Promotions should be personalized based on customers' past history and buying habits. A database system, after one time setup, can automate and personalize all these offers.

Membership

The more often customers come back, the more money you make. If a customer, who used to buy from you once every two months, is now buying from you once a month, you've doubled your business with this customer. As an example, let's say that the once-a-month customer usually purchases a $25 carwash, but you offer him a $50 monthly membership to wash his vehicle as many times as he wants per month, similar as a gym membership. Most customers will not wash their car more than once a week. From a customer's perspective, they got an excellent deal. If they wash once a week, that will be $100 worth of carwashes for half the price. From the operator's point of view, the fixed expenses are the same, the extra expense to wash a car is very minimal, and therefore from an owner perspective the extra $25 is almost one hundred percent profit. Harvard Business School concluded that by increasing customer retention rate by 5%, profit increases between 25-125%. The same principle applies if you increase the frequency of customer visits by 5%.

Loyalty promotions

Offer customers incentives to come back more often to your business or maybe upgrade them to a higher end item. Offer existing customers an incentive to recommend your business to their co-workers, friends, or family to come in and receive a discount.. Offering discount coupons or gift cards with limited time offers can do this. You can also offer discounts to employees of local businesses and give them incentives to recommend their customers to you.

Email

You can use database software to store email addresses and send personalized messages on a regular basis to customers informing them when products that they purchase frequently are on sale. You can also recommend products (based on previously purchased items), and send them incentives to come back.

Social media

Keep in touch with your customers via email, Facebook, and Twitter and other social media. You may announce your specials or you may post humorous stories, pictures or news that may interest them. Those stories have nothing to do with selling your services or products. They are designed to keep you in the mind of your existing clients.

Prepaid cards

Gift cards should be promoted all year long and especially around the holidays. To implement these ideas you need to have a database system for easy control and tracking. Another option is to offer cash cards, which customers can load with any amount they wish and recharge later. Small businesses should offer incentives to purchase gift cards and cash cards for example receive $100 gift card for $90 dollars or prepay for three and get fourth card free.

Smartphone apps

Phone apps for your business are becoming more and more necessary to reach your current clients and motivate them to increase their frequency of visits to your business using the push notification feature. Recent data shows that 74 percent of the phones in the U.S. market are smartphones, up from 58% in 2013. Nielsen reported that two-thirds of phones sold in the second quarter of 2012 were smartphones. According to Nielsen, the vast majority of the primary smartphone users are adults between the ages of 18-54. How many people do you know today that do not have a smartphone?

SMS marketing:

There are approximately 310 million people in the United States. According to www.Comscore.com, about 235 million Americans use mobile devices with text capability.

Text messages cannot increase the frequency of visits unless you take advantage of it by texting great offers. This is especially true during your slow hours or days to entice customers to act immediately on the offer. It is preferred to text an offer not more than once a week, otherwise your clients will opt out.

Here are some more important stats about SMS:

98 percent of SMS are opened and read by recipient.
Mobile phone users look at their phone an average of one hundred fifty times per day.

IV - Control Operational Expenses

The biggest variable expense in many businesses is labor. That can be a big drain on overall profits. A business owner should learn to spot areas to control expenses and increase overall profit. Some expenses should not be cut, such as buying lower quality products to replace high quality products. Add new equipment when possible to speed up overall performance, increase throughput, eliminate bottlenecks, increase overall quality and improve customer satisfaction.

I would highly recommend that you begin managing with facts instead of conjecture by using a data base system dashboard that shows you the pulse of your business at a glance. A dashboard is not intended to show you every conceivable metric, but to show you the key performance indicators in your business. A dashboard keeps what truly matters on your radar screen. It is possible to track key performance indicators such as productivity, speed, efficiency, etc.

It's a sign of a problem when business owners base their business plan on gross income alone. Profit is determined, not by income alone, but by income and expenses combined. Controlling operational expenses should always be a priority for business owners, especially in good times. For profits to show a significant rise, income should go up while expenses per transaction go down. Mistakes happen when business owners try to reduce expenses by eliminating costs in the wrong areas. Imagine a racecar driver installing a smaller engine to save money. If his goal is to win the race, then does it make sense to install a smaller engine? Thus by not maintaining, repairing or installing a piece of equipment that could serve more customers faster and at a lower cost, you are being counter-productive. If you need to attract more customers, would you cut down on advertisement and promotions and the overall look and feel of the business? Landscape, paint, clean restrooms are a minor investment for a greater reward, especially in a slow economy.

CHAPTER 15

The Pillars Foundation

Would you build your house on one pillar? Of course not! Then why would you build your business on one pillar? The stronger the foundation you build, with multiple pillars of marketing strategies, tactical sales, and sound operation procedures, the stronger your business is going to be and the higher your business will soar in a good or bad economy. To gain the unfair advantage, you should have multiple marketing programs to promote your business.

To succeed in business, you need to have a strong foundation. Many people focus too much on how fast and how much they benefit from business instead of first laying a strong foundation for operating proficiently, innovating marketing, strategizing and falling in love with customers. Do you know who your customers really are? Do you know their most critical concerns? If not, how are you going to meet and exceed their expectations?

Take time to understand the most important person in your business—the customer. Learn what they value most, their evolving needs, and be proactive in serving them. It is said that the customer is always right. They have the right to spend their money with whomever they want and on whatever they deem fit. Become a close fit to their expectations and needs.

The needs of your customers always come before your needs. If not, that is a recipe for failure. Your unique value proposition should echo the wishes of your customers. Your UVP should position you in the minds of your customers as being the obvious choice. Learn your competitors' weaknesses and make them your strengths. Research and find out the main complaint customers have in general about your industry, solve it, create your UVP around it, and back it up with a guarantee.

Another way of setting up a good foundation for business is to understand how to manage the income. Cash flow is everything in business. Find a balance between providing value for your customers and making a profit.

Have a system in place to reinvest part of the profits. Treat the business like a baby. It needs nourishment in order to be healthy. You cannot keep taking money from your business without reinvesting and expect it to thrive. To create a sustainable business, you have to keep innovating and add multiple streams of income.

You already know the four levers to increase your business: Increase customer base, increase sales dollar per customer, increase frequency of visits, and control operational expenses. Now how can you use these four levers to help increase your business? First, take each of the four levers and come up with ten different marketing ideas to implement them. Then take each marketing idea and write ten different steps on how to implement it. As you're writing these steps, sometimes the opposite of what you wrote is a better step to implement. Therefore, for every step you write, write down the opposite as well and see if it makes sense.

Root Feeders

Imagine your business as a fruit-bearing tree. The root system of a tree performs many vital functions. Roots transport water and minerals from the soil and anchor the tree to the ground. Root systems consist of larger perennial roots and smaller feeder roots. The small feeder roots constitute the major portion of the root system.

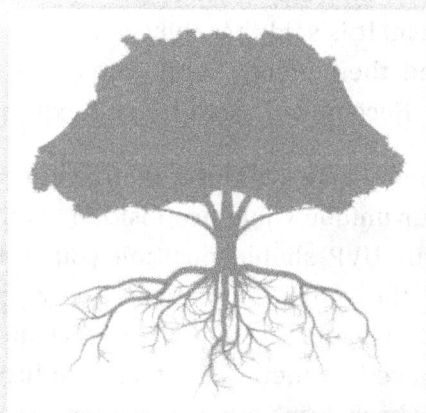

For a tree to grow and produce fruit it has to have strong roots with many feeder roots. The more roots and feeder roots, the stronger the tree grows and the more fruit it will produce. In business, every root represents one strategic marketing idea of a lever to increase profit. Every feeder root represents one tactical step on how to implement the strategic idea. As the tree cannot grow and give fruit with just one root and its feeder roots, likewise your business requires many strategic marketing ideas with at least ten distinctive tactical procedures on how to grow your business exponentially.

Increase Customer Base	Increase Sales $ Per Purchase	Increase Frequency of Visits	Control Operational Expenses

Roots To Increase Customer Base

Promote your Unique Value Proposition
Add multiple streams of income
Customer retention
Referral system
Follow up with potential clients
Follow up with orphan accounts
Create demand and scarcity for your product
Offer a guarantee
Write a book and become the expert of your market
Write a booklet and distribute for free
Acquire new customers at break-even point
Free offers, gift or samples for first time customers
Retrain your salespeople to close more often
Press releases
Email campaign
Blog
Print Advertisement
Social Media
Telemarketing
Use other company's email list to promote you
Partnership with local business
Endorsements from local businesses
Endorsements from celebrities
Fundraising

Join business organizations
Join community events
Exhibits
Trade shows
Networking
Monument sign
Moving sign
Start an education night
Run special events
Fall in love with your customers

Roots To Increase Sales Dollar per Customer

Change your menu and offers.
Change your prices.
Add incentives and value.
Address the wants and needs of your customers.
Retrain salespeople to close sooner and higher.
Stop selling and start educating.
Up-sell and cross-sell.
Package your offers.
Promote your higher packages first.
Visible promotional signs
Point of sale promotions
Prepay for next purchase and save.
Gift certificates and gift cards
Pre-sell your services in packages of three or more
Offer more value with higher packages.
Raise your price.
Offer guarantee or money back
Brochures
Email campaign
Blog
Follow up with customers after sale.
Print Advertisement
Social Media
Visual aids before and after pictures
Testimonial letters
Speed up process
"Wow" service
Gift certificates
Fall in love with your customers

Roots To Increase Frequency of Visits

Promote a membership program.
Prepay for multiple services and save.
Prepay next service at a discount.
Follow up with previous clients.
Pre-sell next service in advance.
Set next appointment or service in advance.
Pre-sell your services in packages of three or more.
Friendly staff
Email campaign
Push notifications
Text messages
Come-back-soon incentives
Speed up efficiency.
Multiple streams of income
Run special events.
Offer a guarantee.
Fall in love with your customers.

Roots To Control Operational Expenses

Systemize process.
Increase productivity.
Upgrade/add equipment.
Eliminate bottlenecks.
Review your policies.
Teamwork
Mission and vision
Sense of urgency
Empower employees
Speed up the process
Apply the Theory Of Limitation.
Fall in love with your customers.

CHAPTER 16

Create Demand and Scarcity

Did you ever go out to a restaurant with friends and families on a Friday night and find it totally empty? Did you feel comfortable going in? Or did you decide to go somewhere else even if you had to wait to be seated? What made you walk out? Most people, when asked why they walked out, give the following reasons:

- Can't trust an empty restaurant.
- Maybe the food isn't good.
- There was no atmosphere.
- They have no business; I don't want to be their first customer.
- Fill in the blank.

The same thing works for many businesses. If you have no customers in the store being served, some customers might hesitate to come in, especially if they are first-time customers. Most people don't want to be the first to try a product or service. I hope now you understand how imperative it is to give incentives to customers to increase their frequency of visits by offering a loyalty program, or to join your automatic renewal memberships if you can offer one. The purpose of the membership is to increase the business income from existing customers; and those customers will also be your filler. In previous chapters, we discussed how expenses become infinite when employees are sitting around waiting for customers and how increasing the frequency of visits from customers at a discounted price might seem below your cost, but in reality it is almost 100 percent profit.

Starbucks

Starbucks prices are very expensive when compared to other coffee shops. Before Starbucks entered the coffee market the cup of coffee was ninety-nine cents. So why do people go to Starbucks?

- Starbucks created an emotional connection with customers.
- Starbucks created the perception that they have the best coffee.

- They offer different selections of coffee drinks and snacks.
- Customers enjoy the great experience and pleasant relaxing atmosphere.
- The friendly Starbucks staff offers quality coffee and builds rapport and trust with their customers.
- Customers see value in the overpriced cup of coffee.
- The result is that their coffee shops are always filled with customers. It became the meeting place for many businesses, and many business transactions are being done over a cup of coffee at Starbucks. Creating demand was no accident, it is a main part of the core marketing plan of Starbucks.

What can you learn from the Starbucks model to gain the unfair advantage?

- Do not re-invent the wheel.
- Copy and improve a successful and proven model.
- Offer customers an unforgettable experience and welcoming atmosphere.
- Build rapport and trust with your customers. Let them feel at home.
- Offer a high quality service that customers are willing to pay for.
- Create value for your product or services and make it a no brainer to do business with you.

Build it and they will come. It is a perception business. If your business is always busy, you must be good. If others trust you, then I can too.

How to Create Demand and Scarcity

A new dentist may instruct his secretary to set all of his appointments on Monday first, and have them over lap by 15 minutes. Once Mondays are full then the secretary can set appointments for Tuesday, and so on.

An attorney may instruct her secretary to always take a message instead of transferring the call and to inform all callers that she is either busy with a client in the office, on the phone with a client, or in court.

A solar company may inform the prospect that they are booked for the next two months with installations and the wait time may get longer because the demand is greater than the supply of the solar panels. It is better to book your time early to start saving money sooner.

An insurance agent, while at a client's house, may inform them that he has five more appointments scheduled and he only has one hour set for this appointment with them.

An auto detail company does not set appointments; instead promotes it services as first come first served. The owner encourages all clients to show up first thing in the morning to reserve their spot for the day.

If you are selling a product or service, add one of the following in big bold letters: While supplies last, limited supply, limited time offer or FREE widget for the first ten customers.

Take advantage of SMS, push notification, or email your current customers with special offers to encourage them to increase the frequency of visits.

- Create a membership program to increase the frequency of visits.

- Offer a loyalty program membership that rewards customers with special discounts and offers.

- The most impressive example of creating an artificial scarcity for something is the diamond business. Diamonds are not rare, they are stored in mass quantities by diamond companies and carefully sold in limited quantities to keep the prices artificially high. It is the principle of supply and demand.

- Offer free samples and demonstrations to increase demand and use the scarcity principle to help you close the deal.

- Write a book or booklet about your industry explaining the potential problem and how your service or product can solve the issue. Distribute the booklet for free to all your existing clients, potential clients and non-competing businesses that their services may complement yours. Doing so will set you as the market expert and create demand for your product or service.

- Become the expert at solving the problems customers have or make them aware of the problem they have that you can solve.

- Start a blog to educate consumers about an existing problem or issue and how your product or service is imperative to solve the issue.

- Become a speaker, authority, coach and a consultant about your product or service.

- Interview experts in your market and their credibility rubs off on you.

- Start an educational seminar or webinar to prospects about a potential problem and the best way to handle it.

- Start a contest and the winner gets...

- Stop selling; start educating to become the authority in your market.

- Start a survey filled with information that helps create an itch, demand and scarcity for your product or service.

- Narrow your target market and dominate that market. You want to be a big fish in a little pond instead of a small fish in a big pond.

CHAPTER 17

Don't Sell, Educate

Because consumers today are more aware of tactical selling techniques, and are quick to build a shield between themselves and sales people, the approach has to change. To gain the unfair advantage, sales methods have to change from tactical to strategic. If you visit an attorney or a doctor, they do not try to sell you; they educate you on the cause of the problem and the available solutions. We are professionals and must act the same way. Thinking strategically opens many doors that were impossible to open when you only worked tactically. Strategic thinking opens the door and makes potential buyers more receptive to hear your message; then you close tactically by asking for the sale.

Be Strategic

Gain the unfair advantage by thinking strategically. As a strategist, you must look at the problem from a global perspective and offer solutions on how to solve the problem. A tactical person calls a company and asks the person in charge if they would be interested in trying a new product.

On the other hand a strategic person may call to do a survey and learn about a company or an industry need. For example, a solar company may call a homeowner and say, "Hi I'm John, the director of market research at XYZ solar company (your title should not include the word sales.)

May I ask you seven quick questions? Are you the homeowner? Do you currently have solar panels on the roof of your house?? Is your electrical bill on the rise? Did you know that electrical costs have risen 40 percent in the last ten years? Did you know your electric company is planning for a 15 percent increase starting January of next year? Did you know you could install solar panels with zero down and cut your current electrical bill by 25 percent to 30 percent immediately? Would you like me to send you some more information?"

This is called educated base marketing. People are more open to learn something that will benefit them instead of listening to a sales call. Perspective reaction to the information you give them should be, "Wow! I did not know that." This approach is ten times more likely to get you into a conversation with the prospect and open more doors for you. If the prospect is interested in additional information about the product, you may say, "I will be headed your direction tomorrow. It would be my pleasure to drop by with some valuable information and show you important facts on how to save money on your electric bill. What's a good time for you?"

With this approach, you are becoming a market expert, not just a product expert. Forget about selling and believe in serving and educating your prospect with information that can help them. This is so prudent because the average prospect is not much of an expert in what you offer, and when you use the educated base marketing strategy, they will consider you an expert in this field and more knowledgeable than any of your competitors. The prospect will trust you more than a tactical person who is just trying to get a sale. What you are doing with this strategy is educating the prospect with good and useful information. You do this by giving them a lot of bad news (pain) to raise their interest in your product or service. This in turn motivates them to open up and be receptive to making a change to get rid of that pain. You are giving them information to motivate them to make a wise decision with their hard earned money.

> *"Insanity is doing the same thing over and over again, but expecting different results."*
> *Albert Einstein*

Peak their Interest

Research done by Chet Holmes, the author of *The Ultimate Sales Machine*, has concluded that about 3 percent of potential buyers are actively looking to buy whatever you are selling. About 7 percent of the consumers are not yet in the buying mode, but they are open to the idea of buying whatever you are selling because they are somewhat dissatisfied with what they already have. The remaining 90 present are divided into three equal categories. Thirty percent are not thinking about purchasing your product or service. Thirty percent don't think they are interested in your product or service, and the last thirty percent are definitely not interested.

Armed with this research, what could you say to have those 90 percent give you a chance and be willing to listen to you? Remember, it is always about the "WIIFM" (what's in it for me) from the customers' perspective. Start by offering them some information that peaks their attention. The information has to be very powerful. Use information that can grab their attention—information that makes them aware of an existing pain, potential pain, or future pain and will make them more receptive to hear your solution.

When you read a newspaper, what makes you read certain articles? Isn't it the title? Do you read the article to get some information that you did not know before? The same idea applies when you are in front of prospects. Give them some information that they did not know to make them stick around to find out the answer.

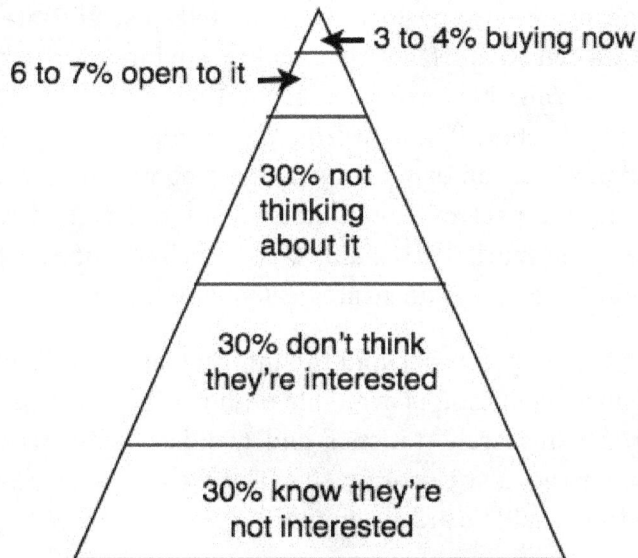

Meet More Prospects

A tactical person will try hard to sell his product and his closing rate will be between 3 and 10 percent because when people feel they are being sold to, they resist. To gain the unfair advantage, a strategic person forgets about selling and works on building a relation with prospects by providing them with "Wow" information that educates them in their personal lives or in business. Instead of calling a business owner and saying, "I can save you money on these widgets," the strategist will say, "I'm the marketing director from XYZ company. This is not a sales call. The reason I'm calling is because we invested thousands of dollars on research to figure out how to prosper in this economy. Our researcher has uncovered five main reasons why 90 percent of all businesses fail within the first ten years. We have also discovered the four dangers facing businesses in the current economy and the nine winning strategies every business should adopt to prosper. Over the next thirty days we will be sharing this information with local small businesses. Would you be interested in learning about the findings of this research?"

There are a few ways to set the meeting. You could have them come to your office, meet them at their office, have a group meeting with many business owners at a local restaurant, or a group meeting in your office for a complimentary lunch and presentation.

During the presentation, do not try to sell, just educate by introducing market data with *pain* facts that makes having your product or service more crucial. Your PowerPoint presentation should be filled with "Wow" data that prospects will benefit from and implement in their business. This will position you as an expert in your field above all your competitors and earn you the respect of your audience. At the end of the presentation, introduce some market data and statistical information that shows how your product or service can strategically benefit them.

Thanks to the computer age and the Internet, all the information needed to create your presentation is available on-line. All it takes is a little research. You may also research statistics and trends of industries, products, and services over the past twenty years. The trends and statistics over a long period of time could be an eye opener.

The following sites may be a good start for your research to create your presentation:

www.gpo.gov
www.census.gov
www.stats.bls.gov
www.nhtsa.gov
www.fedstats.gov

www.uspto.gov
www.archive.org
www.ropercenter.uconn.edu
www.gallup.com
www.jdpower.com
www.dnb.com
www.deloitte.com
www.exchange.aaa.com
www.ceoexpress.com
www.socialnomics.net

> *"People don't care how much you know,
> until they know how much you care."*

CHAPTER 18

The Speed of Innovation

Wayne Gretzky was once asked, "How can you be the best hockey player if you're not the strongest or fastest player?" He responded, "Most players go where the puck is, I go where the puck is going to be." As a business owner, your job is to anticipate change in the industry and be ahead of the competition. I've heard it many times, "Ask customers what they want and give it to them." That is called meeting their expectations. In reality, customers don't know what they want until you offer it to them—that is called exceeding their expectations.

Your goal should be to become a master of change, rather than a victim of change. Technology moves so fast today that sometimes it's tempting to just throw up your hands and say, "I'll never get up to speed." Well, your business can't afford that attitude. Today's technology is essential to give your small business the edge over the competitors.

Innovation matters now more than ever. The only way the United States is able to compete with the developing world that offer lower cost products and services is by constantly innovating. The top five innovative companies in the world per Boston Consulting Group for 2013 are:

1. Apple, U.S.
2. Samsung, South Korea
3. Google, U.S.
4. Microsoft, U.S.
5. Toyota, Japan
6. IBM, U.S.
7. Amazon, U.S.
8. Ford, U.S.
9. BMW, Germany
10. General Electric, U.S.

As you can see, companies from United States dominate the list. Apple, the first company to come to mind when talking about innovation doesn't compete on price. It doesn't lower prices to attract more customers. Instead it innovates itself out of its predicament.

Cheap labor and low cost manufacturing have driven the rise of China and India as emerging market powerhouses to date. But they are no longer content to be the world's factory. They are rapidly realizing that innovation is the key to turn into developed countries.

> *"Sometimes when you innovate, you make mistakes. It is best to admit them quickly, and get on with improving your other innovations."*
>
> *Steve Jobs*

Professor Amar Bhide in his book *The Origin and Evolution of New Businesses* showed that 93 percent of all companies that ultimately became successful were open minded and realized, before it was too late that their original strategy they founded the business on had to be changed. To gain the unfair advantage, change your business model to be an innovator. Why? Because the odds are against you unless you do something about it. Here are the facts according to *Entrepreneur Magazine*:

- 30 percent of companies fail within the first year.
- 70 percent of companies fail within five years.
- 90 percent of small businesses fail within ten years.
- 85 percent of businesses that succeed never reach the million-dollar mark.
- 95 percent of those businesses never reach the five million dollar mark.
- 90 percent of franchises succeed over ten years!

Why is it that 90 percent of franchises succeed over ten years as opposed to 90 percent of small businesses fail within the same time?

The answer is that franchisees have to follow systems created by their franchisors. The franchisors invest millions of dollars innovating and systemizing their processes.

The reality is business models are in constant change. It is no longer true that an entrepreneur can use one single business model to manage his entire operation or use the same model he inherited from the generation before. Today is a different reality from a few years ago. The technology and Internet revolution has changed the way we do business. Constant change, innovation, and strategizing are essential today. Who said you have to operate your business the same way as your competitors do? Sometimes the opposite of the traditional way of doing business is more profitable. Think out of the box. Change is not only mandatory; it is profitable. Learn from businesses that innovated and drove others to perish.

> *You can't just ask customers what they want and then try to give that to them. By the time you get it built, they'll want something new.*
>
> *Steve Jobs*

Netflix

Hollywood Video and Blockbuster were both leading stores for renting movies and video games. They had a great business model for the 1990s when they had a virtual monopoly on the market. But in the new century the game changed when Netflix stole the market by innovating. Hollywood Video and Blockbuster have been *netflixed*. *Netflixed* is a new verb used by entrepreneurs. It means to have a previously successful business model destroyed by a new, innovative business model. Netflix did not invent any new technology; instead they innovated by changing the business model. Netflix created a virtual world and introduced the monthly subscription model with unlimited rentals without due dates, late fees or shipping fees. Netflix developed a personalized video recommendation system based on ratings and reviews by its customers. Hollywood Video and Blockbuster kept the same old business model and did not innovate. Hollywood Video filed bankruptcy in May 2010, and announced the end of operation and liquidated all its assets. Blockbuster also announced bankruptcy in

September 2010, and Dish Network purchased it in an auction in April 2011.

As innovative as Netflix was, a further evolution took place just a few years later through a company called Redbox. Instead of having a monthly subscription, Redbox offers a non-subscription movie rental service for one dollar per movie. Redbox has now taken a big share of Netflix's market because they innovated by cutting down operational expenses and passing the savings to their prospects.

> *"Pretty much, Apple and Dell are the only ones in this industry making money. They make it by being Walmart. We make it by innovation."*
>
> *Steve Jobs*

Apple

Steve Jobs did not invent the personal computer, MP3, smart phone or tablet computer. Yet he innovated all of these devices and became the leader of the industry. Steve Jobs changed the game by innovating and introducing new and improved products year after year.

Learn from others to innovate and be passionate about what you do or get out of the business. When people ask me what I do for a living I answer, "I never worked a day in my life." When you are passionate about what you do, then it is not work. George Burns said, "I would rather fail at something I love to do than succeed at something I hate."

Questions to Ponder

If you start looking where no one else is looking, you can see what no one else is seeing, so you can do what no one else is doing. One of my favorite quotes comes from Andrew Grove, the retired CEO of Intel: "Only the paranoid survive." As mentioned previously, every time Intel invents a new chip they already have a team trying to make that chip obsolete. Why? Because if they don't someone else will. That's the same mentality all business owners should have. Therefore, owners should work to stay ahead of the competition by asking themselves on a daily basis the following questions:

- What differentiates me from the competition?
- How can I reduce labor cost?
- How can I bring the best out in the employees? After all, happy employees equal happy customers.
- What incentives can I give customers to come back and come back more often?
- How can I lower my prices and increase dollars per transaction at the same time?
- What can I do to improve overall quality?
- Why should customers choose my business over the competition?
- How can I improve on what I've been doing right?
- How can I do more of what I've been doing right?
- How can I exceed customers' expectations even more?
- What are customers' biggest concerns and how can I resolve them?
- How can I increase the number of customers per man-hour (productivity)?
- What are the bottlenecks in our system and how can I resolve the issues?
- How can I increase our total number of clients?
- What values do I offer my clients that the competition cannot?
- How can I increase the value I already give my clients?
- How can I "Wow" customers every step of the way?
- What kind of experience do customers get at the business and how can I improve it?
- What experiences do I like from other industries that I can adopt and implement at my business?
- How can I make the experience of doing business with us more enjoyable and memorable?
- How can I change my business philosophy from sales driven to educational driven?
- How can I improve our image?
- How can I innovate?
- How can I change the game?

To gain the unfair advantage, entrepreneurs should always read trade magazines from all types of industries and scan for new ideas to implement.

Read business and marketing books. Visit successful businesses in the industry and learn the secret of their success. Study the secrets of success and innovative ideas of other industries and adapt them to your industry. Commit to excellence because "Good isn't good enough. Good is the enemy of great."

> *"To get what you want in life, help enough other people get what they want first."*

SECTION VI

THE TACTICAL PRINCIPLE

CHAPTER 19

Nothing Changes
If Nothing Changes

The fastest way to increase profit is to increase dollars per transaction. To do so you must first re-work your offers and bundle your offers and add higher end product or service. Promote the savings of buying in bundle versus a la carte. Keep the offers you present to clients between three and four. The highest and best service that you want to promote the most should be the first offer you present. Retrain your managers and employees on the new menu and how to become educated base professional salespeople.

When you get sick and go to the doctor, the first thing the doctor does is ask you questions about your symptoms. He listens to your answers, takes notes, and then he runs some tests to come up with a diagnosis. Afterwards, he offers you options to resolve the problem and recommends the best solution in his professional opinion.

The same is true if you have a legal problem. The attorney asks you questions, listens to your answers, takes notes, comes up with different plans to resolve the issue; and then using his professional expertise, recommends the best solution.

The only difference between an entrepreneurial business and the health and legal professions, is that when clients visit their doctors or attorneys, they already know they have a problem, which is causing them a lot of pain, either physically or financially. Salespeople need to make customers aware of the potential pain to the customer if they don't invest in your product or service today by:

- Asking the proper questions
- Listening to answers
- Asking more leading questions

- Educating the customer on the cause of their problem and the consequences.
- Running tests, give samples or a demonstration
- Offering solutions
- Recommending the best solution
- Presenting letters or video from passed clients who had the same issues
- Creating sense of urgency
- Giving incentives to have a product or service purchased immediately

Salespeople today have to be educators. To motivate your salespeople, pay them on an escalated commission based on dollars per transaction. Salespeople have to see themselves as self-employed business owners. The more they sell the more they make. Their income depends on their selling ability and their motivation to go out and talk to potential clients. The more they sell, the more commission they make. They have to see the business customers as their own clients. Once they do, the salespeople will build relationships with the customers and strive to exceed their expectations; which will keep the customers coming back and encourage them to refer many of their friends, coworkers and family members.

Training should include advice on how to handle rejection. Receiving too many negative responses from customers normally makes salespeople withdraw, procrastinate, and avoid talking to customers. Many average salespeople have a fear of rejection; therefore, they avoid talking to customers about what their needs are. Untrained salespeople assume the answer will be no. They think the word "No" is a bad word. Professional salespeople have the obligation and duty to educate the consumer on the need for the product or service necessary to protect their investments or enhance their lives. If they do not, everyone loses; your clients, your company, and the salesperson.

> *"Sales are in direct proportion to how many times you hear the word 'no' before you get a 'yes.'"*

Love the Word "No"

The word we use most with young children is no. As a result, the word *no* is one of the first words we learn. As we grow, we use the word *no* as a defensive mechanism. The word *no* is a reaction we often exhibit without thinking. For example, when I go to a department store looking to buy some clothes, and someone approaches me and asks, "Can I help you find something?" My first answer is, "No, thank you." Why? Because *no* does not require any thought and it is a subconscious protection from those salespeople who are trying to take some of my hard earned money. It is already embedded in my head as a defensive mechanism against salespeople. The same is true when you are trying to sell products or services to your customers. The word *no* is only a reaction. However, you need to realize that every *no* you hear gets you one step closer to a *yes*.

For example, let us assume for simplicity's sake, that you get *no* nine times before you get one *yes*. Let's also assume that every *yes* is equal to $100, that means for the first nine customers you talk to and they decline to buy your service, they each hypothetically forward their $10 to the tenth person who pays you at the end for the service. Though you have not received the money yet, you should really thank the first nine customers for giving you the opportunity to show them what you believe they need to save them future pain. (The pain technique will be discussed later.) You should thank them in your mind for the $10 they paid to the tenth customer. And, if you feel you pressured a customer and made him feel uncomfortable, I would advise you to apologize. A professional salesperson should never use high-pressure tactics. What a professional person does is lead the clients through questions and give them information to help them make the right decision.

Thomas Edison

Thomas Edison conducted more than ten thousand experiments before he invented the light bulb. During an interview, Napoleon Hill asked Edison, "You failed over ten thousand times. How did you feel after every time you failed?" Edison replied, "I did not fail ten thousand times. I learned ten thousand approaches on how not to invent the light bulb." When asked to clarify, Edison said, "I ran out of ideas that do not work and I learned from every experiment, and every experiment got me one step closer to inventing it."

For Edison, every failure was a learning experience. The same is true in sales. Every time you get a *no* ask yourself:

What did I do right?

What did I do wrong?

What can I learn from the experience to help me do better next time?

Ty Cobb

Ty Cobb was one of the best base stealers in the history of professional baseball. In one season he stole ninety-six bases out of one hundred forty-four attempts. He was successful 66 percent of the time and was inducted into the Baseball Hall of Fame because of his record. Another baseball player, Max Carry, was over 90 percent successful at stealing bases, but he is not in the Hall of Fame. Why? Was that a mistake? The answer is simple. Because, in his best season, Carry stole fifty-one bases out of only fifty-three attempts. He did not take enough chances. In life you are not recognized for the percentage of times you failed, but rather by the number of times you succeeded.

> *"In life, you are not judged by how many times you fail, but by how many times you succeed. And success is in direct proportion to how many times you fail but keep on trying."*
> *Tom Hopkins*

Babe Ruth

Babe Ruth's 714 career home-runs ranks him among the best of all time, but people tend to forget he struck out 1,330 times or 66 percent of all his attempts. Ruth finished his career with a 342 batting average. Babe Ruth was successful at hitting the ball only 34 percent of the time.

To Upgrade or Not to Upgrade

Selling products or services is similar to selling a car at a dealership. When a person wants to buy a car, they research which cars they like, and then go to a dealer with the intention of buying a vehicle. It's just a matter of finding the right vehicle. Let's say a customer goes to a car dealership with a

$20,000 budget. A good salesperson can sell the customer a vehicle with a few perks for $24,000. That's only 20 percent above their budget. It is possible to also do this in small retail stores, carwashes, solar companies or restaurants. A restaurant server may suggest an appetizer, alcoholic beverage, or soft drinks. Servers may also suggest a desert. Better yet, the server carries a tray with all desert samples on it to show customers and have them choose the one they would like to try. The same with a solar company, they may suggest to install enough panels to keep the bill at tier one, or they may give them the option to invest in more panels today and not worry about paying a penny to the electric company. Upgrading many customers just 10 percent to 20 percent above their initial budget is relatively easy and can greatly increase overall profits.

In some cases it is harder, but still possible to upgrade customers, if they came in for one item and are tried to be sold on something totally different. For example, in the case of the car wash, a customer comes in for a wash and is offered a car detailing. They had no intention of having their vehicle detailed. For simplicity of calculation, let's say a customer comes in for a $10 carwash, but you upgrade him to a $200 detail. That is a 2,000 percent increase over his budget and it's not what the customer came in for. The steps on how to upgrade customers will be handled later in the chapter. I've had some former car sales people come to work for me, and they all had difficulty upgrading customers from a carwash to detail service. Eventually they all quit. On the other hand, one of my carwash salespeople went to work for a car dealership and within two months he had become their top salesperson.

I learned the following sayings from the Tom Hopkins Learning Library and Live Boot Camp Seminars. Tom Hopkins had us memorize these sayings and we had a test the last day of the seminar. So here they are. I encourage you to memorize them and use them.

I don't see failure as failure but as a learning experience.
Do what you fear most and you conquer fear.
I don't see failure as failure, only as a negative feedback I need to learn from and change course in my direction.
I don't see rejection as a rejection, only as an opportunity to practice my techniques so I can get better.
I don't see rejection as a failure, only as a percentage game I must play to win.

You are not remembered by the number of times you fail but by the number of times you succeed.

I am not judged by the number of times I get rejected but by the number of times I succeed, and the number of times I succeed is in direct proportion to the number of times I fail and keep on trying.

To Train or Not to Train

The following is an example to help you understand how much lack of training and the fear of rejection can cost your business.

Let's say on average, for every twenty customers the sales representative talks to about upgrading a product or service, he closes one sale. There are twenty customers per hour who visit the business for service, yet because the salesperson is afraid of rejection, it takes him four hours of picking and choosing to talk to these twenty customers about upgrading to a much better service. That means the salesperson is talking to only five customers per hour. What if, with correct training, salespeople talk to the twenty customers in two hours? What if they were able to use features and benefits to up-sell customers and increase the average sale from $150 to $200? Let's look at the following chart:

Hour	Number of customers	Before training	After training
1	20		
2	40		$200
3	60		
4	80	$150	$200
5	100		
6	120		$200
7	140		
8	160	$150	$200
Total Sales		$300	$800

172

Before training, it took four hours to talk to 20 customers. With training, it takes two hours to talk to 20 the customers. What happened eight hours later? **A 266 percent return on investment**. With properly trained salespeople, dollar per customer grows exponentially, while your sales representative is talking to the same number of people every day. With the proper training, salespeople can overcome rejections, lead customers to make the right decisions, and hopefully, close the fifteenth customer to invest in the products or services instead of the twentieth customer.

It is a numbers game! Closing a sale has ratios. It is part of the Law of Averages. Eventually, as salespeople are trained and develop their skills, the ratio will improve. The goal is to move them from being a novice tactical salesperson to being an expert strategic and tactical salesperson. When this is done, the closing ratio will improve, as well as the dollar per transaction. In the past, prospects would average six "no's" before saying "yes." Today, prospects are savvier and have better resistance to salespeople. Today, an average prospect may say, "No" eight times before a "Yes." Unfortunately, most untrained sales personnel stop after hearing the first or second "no" and don't persist long enough for the law of averages to work in their favor. In the following chapter you will learn how to create demand and scarcity for your product or service, and how to stop selling and start educating, along with other strategic and tactical ideas to help lower customers' resistance and improve your closing ratio.

Is training sales staff an expense or is it an investment? Unfortunately, when I ask many business owners to invest in training their salespeople, they respond by saying they can't afford it. They look at the training as an expense. I show them the above chart then ask the following questions:

Can you afford not to train your sales staff?

Wouldn't you rather have a trained person working for you to increase your profit exponentially?

Some owners shock me with their responses when they say that the reason they don't invest in training their sales people is because they are afraid that after the training, the salespeople will leave them for a better opportunity or better pay. My answer is, employees normally leave for the following reasons:

- They are not being treated right.
- They are not happy at their current job.
- Their current position has no future.
- They would like to make more money.

If you already treat them right what about the other conditions?

Why are they not happy?

Does it have to do with how much money they make?

Is there a future in the current position without proper training?

Can you afford to pay them more if they don't produce more?

Isn't it more like, if they were properly trained their sales would improve, and therefore, they would make more money?

If they made more money wouldn't they feel better and change their perspective about working for you?

Improving your revenue is a win-win for both of you, isn't it?

And if that was not enough to convince the person, then I ask:

Do you drive a car?

Do you drive 50 or 60 miles per hour?

Are you committed to driving on your side of the road and not crossing over the yellow line and hitting the opposite cars head on?

How do you know if the other drivers are committed to doing the same?

You have to commit to doing what is right for you, your company, and your employees, regardless of the other person. Isn't that the truth?

Life is about cause and effect, action and reaction. Mahatma Gandhi said it best with the following quote:

> *"Be the change you want to see in the world."*
> *Mahatma Gandhi*

CHAPTER 20

The Root Feeders

This chapter will cover how to take one idea and implement it to increase your sales dollar per transaction. As mentioned previously, a tree cannot grow without roots and its feeders. The idea to train salespeople is the root, and the feeders are the how-to steps.

The how-to steps to close more sales more often are:

1. Dress for success
2. Use body language and tone of voice
3. Build rapport
4. Identify the problem
5. Don't sell, educate
6. Use pain and pleasure emotional triggers
7. Give samples and explain process
8. Trigger emotional senses
9. Ask questions
10. Defuse tension
11. Don't make the price the main issue
12. Build value
13. Remember "No" doesn't mean "No"
14. Find the last objection, isolate it, then solve it
15. Offer incentives and establish a sense of urgency
16. Close the sale (open a relationship)
17. Silence means consent
18. Up-sell and cross-sell using features and benefits
19. Sell them in bunches like bananas
20. Use gift certificates
21. Ask for referral
22. Follow up
23. Ask for testimony letters

Sales Anatomy

1. Dress for success.

You cannot make a first impression the second time around. A first impression is the first key for any relationship, especially when it comes to business. The first and most important step is dressing for success. When customers go into any business and see employees in mismatched outfits, they are not going to respect them as much as somebody who is clean shaven and wearing a clean uniform. *Perception* is the key word here. For example, a customer perceives a well-dressed salesman as self-confident and knowledgeable. Then, when compared to a less eye-catching business, yours will be thought of as the more professional, organized and successful of the two.

At my carwash business, I had some salespeople dress with a suit and tie on a regular basis. It was so impressive that many customers who knew them were very impressed and many other customers thought they were the owners of the carwash. On the days they wore suits their sales per car were higher than the average days. Image is everything. You don't have a second chance to make a first impression.

2. Use body language.

Body language is essential in business dealings. For example, the manner in which a person walks is very important. Walk with your head up, shoulders back, and a smile on your face. A smile gives the impression of confidence, happiness, and friendship, and is a non-verbal signal that you recognize the customer you're greeting. The speed you walk also has an unspoken meaning, as does the volume of your voice. Walk fast enough so as to neither be running nor walking too slowly. This non-verbal communication tells the customer you are here to serve them, and it shows enthusiasm.

n 1963, Albert Mehrabian, a psychology professor at UCLA, performed a study on how people decide whether to buy from a salesperson or not. Mehrabian was seeking to understand the relative impact of facial expressions and spoken words. He concluded that a person's decision to buy from a salesperson is based on the following formula:

55 percent on body language.
38 percent on tone of voice.
7 percent on the words spoken.

Look at the above percentages. Only 7 percent buy from you because of what you say and 93 percent buy because of what you didn't say. Body language and tone of voice work both ways. Your body language can influence a customer's decision and gives them subconscious messages as to whether they should trust you or not. Just imagine how many sales you would gain if your body language communicated trust and concern.

Send the right message. On average, a person speaks between 100 to 150 words per minute. On the other hand, a person can listen to 400 words per minute. What does that mean? It means, that when you are speaking to someone at one 100 words per minute, that person has enough time to criticize your body language and tone of voice, among other things, and form an opinion about you.

Mirroring your customer's body language subconsciously sends a message to the prospect that you are the same. Learn to speak the language of your potential client. Each person has a style and uses certain words when speaking based on their level of education and backgrounds. Pick up on words they use most and use them in your conversation. Pace the speed and match their volume and tone of voice. Think about it for a second. Who are your friends? What kind of habits do they have? How do they behave? What about their tone of voice and body language? Aren't they, in most cases, a mirror of you?

Learn to read body language. What a customer says could be different from what he is thinking. That's why observing and understanding body language is critical. Prospects may lie, but their body language always speaks the truth, which is why we can never rely on their words alone. The wrong place to look for body language is the face because people can manipulate their facial expressions and hide their true feeling and opinion. The right place to look is the direction of the feet, hips, hand motions and overall body movements. The reason why is the body movements are controlled subconsciously and reflect the honest opinion about the subject at hand. I recommend you read books about body language to gain the unfair advantage.

A smile is one of your most powerful tools. Some companies install mirrors next to their phones and require all staff members to look at the mirror and smile before answering the phone call. Smiling changes the way you sound completely. Have you ever been in a shouting match with your spouse or child and the phone started ringing? When you picked up the phone, did you scream at the caller? Or, did your facial expression flip to a big smile as you answered in a sincere warm voice? This is what everyone should do when meeting a prospect. Always remember that your customers are not customers all day long or every day of the week. That is not what they do for a living. They work just like you and me and are always under pressure from their bosses and their customers. They have seen enough of grumpy people at their work. They expect the best and friendliest service to be given to them. They expect to be given the warmest welcome; otherwise their expectations will not be met and their loyalty will slip away.

3. Build rapport.

People hate to be sold, but love to buy from people they trust. When you meet a prospect for the first time, they build an invisible wall between the two of you that prevents you from selling them anything. Building rapport and a relationship with the customer will break this hidden wall and put you on their good side, so you can work together to make the best choice for their benefit. Building rapport is equivalent to building trust in a friendship.

People are more receptive to people like themselves. Focus on learning your customers' names to make them feel as special as can be. A name is the first thing a person owns and the only thing that will stay with them their whole life and no one can take it away from them. Try to finish off your statement by mentioning the person's name. By doing so, their mood will become more positive. If you can change the mood of your customer, they will buy with emotion.

Why not use every tool possible to put the customer in the listening mood and be interested in what you are saying? As long as you build relationships with customers, they are no longer customers—they become friends and family members.

Creating a solid foundation of trust and friendship is a very critical and important step that is frequently overlooked. Find something in common between yourself and your client, or something the customer is interested in talking about that makes him feel comfortable so he opens up to you. For example is there a local or national news story about sports, weather, or popular culture? Talk to your prospects as if they are your close friends. You must be sincere in being interested in them, because your body language will be sending out subconscious signals.

> *"To build rapport, learn to be interested, not interesting!"*

A good practice is to use your senses accordingly. You have two ears and one mouth, so you should listen twice as much as you speak. Ask questions and let the customer talk while you listen then ask even more questions. People love to talk, especially if the subject is dear to their hearts. I remember one time in 1997—after I researched how to mirror and build rapport — one of my salespeople asked me to help close a sale. He said the customer's car needed to be detailed, but he couldn't convince him to do it today. I decided to test my new mirroring and rapport building techniques with this prospect.

I approached the customer at the waiting area, introduced myself and asked him if everything was okay. I acknowledged that my salesperson mentioned to me that he talked to him about detailing his vehicle. Then I changed the subject and asked him about what he does for a living. Then we talked about his hobbies. He loved fishing. He has a motor home that he uses for vacationing and fishing trips. When we talked about fishing, I could see his face light up. I mirrored his emotion, enthusiasm, tone of voice, and body language. I kept asking him questions about fishing, showing interest, and he kept talking.

Ten minutes later, the customer said, "I really enjoyed talking to you. My motor home needs to be detailed as well. If I leave my car here now can you give me a ride home and give me an estimate on the motor home?" To make a long story short, the customer ended up paying $750 that day.

Pacing, mirroring, and rapport building work like magic and should not be abused. By just learning and implementing these techniques, you'll notice a better close ratio and an increase in sales dollars per transaction. To summarize, "Be interested, not interesting." Have a sincere interest in what your prospect has to say. Pay attention to your body language so you do not give negative subconscious messages. Watch your prospects' body language to know if they are interested in what you are saying. Talk less and listen more. Ask open-ended questions to keep them talking about their interests. Do the customers talk loudly or softly? Do they talk quickly or slowly? Mind the tone of your voice and its speed and volume. Mirror the body language but don't make it obvious. If they cross their hands, cross your legs. If they move their hands as they are talking, move yours when you talk. If they nod their head, nod yours in agreement. Eye contact is very important. Match their facial expression instantly. Assume you already have rapport—talk to them as if you are already good friends.

Building rapport is also an essential step in handling customer complaints. Use the same technique above. First, acknowledge the customer's problem, assure her that you will help resolve the issue, then change the subject to find something of interest to the customer to talk about until she calms down.

> "Prospects must like you and trust you
> before they are willing to listen to you."

4. Identify the problem.

As we discussed earlier, when customers visit a carwash they usually have no clue that their vehicle has a problem that needs to be corrected in order to protect their car's finish and/or interior. Many customers don't even realize that these problems can be fixed at their local carwash. Most ticket writers don't bother trying to identify the customer's automobile issues and go straight to asking for the detail. This is a big mistake.

Put yourself in the customer's shoes. If you pull into a carwash and the ticket writer says, "We have a special on detailing your vehicle," how would you feel and what would you think? You automatically build an invisible wall between you and the salesperson because you feel that he is just trying to sell you something you don't need and take your hard-earned money.

> *"People don't buy a product for the sake of the product.*
> *They buy the solution the product provides."*

5. Don't sell, educate.

Another big mistake salespeople make is concentrating on the finished product instead of educating customers on the reasons they need the product. They should, instead, be educating the customer on what caused the problem. (Chapter 17, "Don't sell, Educate" is dedicated for this subject.) Consumers don't just buy a product or service, they buy what the product or service does for them. They buy solution, comfort, safety, sensation, and status. Many customers don't realize that they are going to face problems in the future and that your service or product is the solution. As a salesperson educate the customer on their current problem and the potential troubles they will face in the future. This could also apply to enhancing the customer's purchase or experience with the appropriate supplemental product or service. Many times this is not known without the proper education. At the carwash, we educate on what causes the car to oxidize and lose it's shine. We educate on how acid rain, industrial fall out, bird droppings, and tree sap damage the paint finish. Then we explain the process of how we can repair the damage and prevent more damage in the future. The education makes you the authority on the subject, sets you as the expert in the market and gives you the unfair advantage. It makes clients most likely to trust you to perform the service if they chose to go ahead. What about your service or product? Can you educate on the process and benefit?

6. Use pain and pleasure emotional triggers.

People are driven by their emotions. We make decisions based on emotions, and then we defend those decisions logically. Understanding those emotions and how to trigger them will help you gain the unfair advantage. We are driven by two different core emotions—pain and pleasure. Pain is a much stronger motivator than pleasure. We seek pleasure and avoid pain.

Therefore, we must show customers that doing nothing today is painful and will cause them a greater pain in the future, and making a decision today will give them immediate pleasure. The subconscious mind plays a big role in decision-making. The subconscious mind is very lazy—it doesn't like change and goes into a defensive mechanism to avoid what it believes is danger.

What would you do if someone threw a ball of fire at you? Would you take a minute to think or would you simply react instinctively to protect yourself? Now, what if you got home from a long day at work and you were looking forward to relaxing? Once you arrived home your wife says she has a surprise for you. She has hired a babysitter for the kids so the two of you can go out to dinner and see a movie. You are really looking forward to seeing the movie and sharing a nice meal with your wife at your favorite restaurant, but you're very tired. Would you try to talk your wife out of it?

Don't get me wrong. Pleasure is a great motivation to have customers act on. I use pleasure almost as much as I use pain. But the pleasure emotion has to be so powerful that the person thinks he wants what you are selling—not just needs it. I normally shoot pain, pain and more pain at the customer, and then when they have enough pain I offer pleasure to get them out of that pain. In other words, I make them aware of the problem. I explain to them that doing nothing will make the problem worse and cause more pain. Then I remind them how much pleasure they had in the past before the problem existed, which causes more pain, and then I offer a solution (pleasure).

Pleasure has to be strong enough to make the customer *want* something instead of just *need* something. We all need a car for transportation, but why do many people buy a Mercedes Benz and pay $100,000 for it instead of purchasing a Kia for a few thousand dollars? Choosing a car's make, model, and color is an emotional decision (want). Transportation is a logical decision (need).

I will share a story from my carwash business. I have trained my cashiers, as well as my salespeople, on how to sell our auto-renewal wash passes. One day as I was walking by the cashier, I heard her and another salesperson trying to sell a wash membership to a customer. The customer had just brought in her brand new vehicle for our $25 wash package. The

182

membership for the same package is $50 per month for unlimited washes. They were trying to convince the customer by saying, "For another $25 today you can wash your car as many times as you want per month and you may cancel anytime you want, no strings attached, after the first two months." The customer was unreceptive and they finally gave up. As the customer was getting ready to pay for her wash, I said,

"May I ask you a question?"

"Yes," she replied.

"When did you buy the vehicle?"

"Last week."

"Isn't it a great feeling every time you get in your new car to drive?"

"Yes."

"Before you purchased this vehicle, what kind of car did you have?"

"Xyz vehicle."

"Did you buy it brand new?"

"Yes."

"Do you remember when you bought it you had the same feelings that you're having today?"

"Yes."

"What happened six months later? Did you lose that feeling?"

"Yes."

"The reason we developed this VIP membership is for new car owners like yourself, who enjoy their car and want to keep it clean and shiny the way you have it today, and five years from today. Every time you get in your car you'll feel great and say, "Wow", I love my car.'"

"Where do I sign?" she replied.

What's the difference between my approach and the cashier's? The cashier and salesperson were trying to sell the customer logically. Logically, if a customer washes her car at least twice a month she gets her money back. If she washes once a week then she'll be getting the carwash at half price. But all that doesn't matter—because when you sell logically, the customers build an invisible wall between you and themselves, and they feel you are trying to sell them for your own benefit and not theirs. What I did was use an emotional trigger. Basically, I asked her, "Do you want those emotions to last and stay with you as long as you own the car?" The obvious answer is, "Yes." I reminded her of today's pleasure, the feelings of owning a new vehicle, and the great feeling she experiences every time she gets into her car. I triggered the fear in her of losing the current pleasurable emotion when I reminded her of how she had the same feeling with her previous car, but that feeling only lasted for about six months because the car no longer looked new. I used emotion triggers, pain and pleasure. She loved the pleasure feeling and wanted it to last forever, but she also felt the pain of losing that feeling.

Another story. I was in the wash tunnel watching cars exit when I saw a salesperson get into a car and drive it out. He told me he was taking the car to the detail area to sell the customer an interior steam clean, and he asked me if I would help him close the deal. I waited a few minutes then followed him to the detail area. When I got there, the customer was ready to leave. I asked, "What's going on?" The salesman told me he offered the interior steam clean to the customer for $150 but the customer changed his mind and was leaving. I asked the customer to wait a second. I opened the vehicle doors to see the condition and how much work it would take us to do the job. As I opened the back door I saw a baby seat. I turned to the customer and said, "May I ask you a question?"

"Yes."

"Do you sometimes get in your car and, after you close the door and turn the engine on, you feel as if you just got an allergy?"

"Yes," he said.

"Did you know that in every one square yard of carpet there are one hundred thousand dust mites populating? Every dust mite produces 20 droppings a day. That is a total of two million dust mites and dust mite dropping lurking in every one square yard of carpet. Did you know that every speck of dust we inhale has approximately forty thousand dust mites and dust mite droppings? That is the cause of your allergy. If you feel the allergy when you get into your vehicle, what about that child in the back seat?"

"Would you include the carwash price in the cost of the steam clean??" he asked.

184

I looked toward the salesman and told him to have the detailer start on the steam clean and make the ticket with credit for the wash. Then I looked at the customer, shook his hand and assured him he would be very happy with the quality of work.

What happened here? I educated the customer about a problem using the emotional trigger called fear. Who would want their baby to suffer from allergies if they can prevent it?

Note: When the customer asked me a conditional question (Would you include the carwash price with the steam clean?), he was telling me that if I included the wash with the detail he would do it. I did not have to confirm it. I just accepted his condition and looked at my salesman and asked him to start the job and print the ticket.

One more story. One morning as I came to work, a salesperson handed me a piece of paper with a customer's name and phone number on it. He said that he tried to sell the customer a $300 detail, but the customer refused to pay that much and asked for a discount. The salesman asked me to call the customer and help close the deal. I called the customer and the first thing he asked me after I introduced myself was, "How much of a discount are you going to give me to detail my vehicle?"

I asked him to come in and let me look at the vehicle, as I could not make a decision on the phone without seeing the vehicle's condition. I assured him he would be happy and I would make sure of that. When the customer came in, I went out to inspect the vehicle. The rear fiberglass bumper was oxidized and I saw the clear coat had just started to peel. After further inspection, I saw on the top of the car next to the rear windshield, a very oxidized section. I educated the customer on what causes clear coat contamination, damage, and peeling. I explained why cars should always be clayed, buffed, and waxed to protect their finishes. I asked for permission to buff a sample on the bumper. After we buffed the sample, I showed him where the paint already peeled and told him there was nothing we could do about it. Then I pointed to the very oxidized section on the roof and said that I wasn't sure if buffing this section would work. If clear coat is peeling, then it's too late, because the process of the clear coat losing adhesion with the paint had begun. It would cost about $1,500 to repaint the car to its original paint quality. I clayed the area, then picked up the buffer and slowly buffed the area. I took my time buffing to keep the customer wondering. Once I was done, the area was very shiny and looked like a showroom finish. That's when I saw the sense of relief in the face of the customer. Then the customer asked me, "How much of a discount are you going to give me?"

I looked at him and said, "Sorry, I cannot discount anything because the paint is in such bad shape, and in order to restore it, it will take more time than an average vehicle."

The customer said, "Okay, go ahead and start on it."

In this situation I used two emotional triggers—fear and relief. The fear of losing the clear coat and spending about $1,500 to repaint the car, and the relief of, "Wow!" (Pleasure), the paint is still in good enough shape that it can be saved.

7. Give free samples or present a demonstration and explain the process.

We don't sell customers; we lead them to make the right decision. If you tell them, they doubt it—if they see it, they believe it. This is the reason successful stores, such as Apple, allow customers to try the product first. Apple has most of their products out for customers to handle and test before purchasing. They also have well trained employees to help customers understand how the product features work. This builds credibility and shows that the product works as advertised. It triggers emotions and increases the odds that customers will purchase the product, because they are now more confident in the product. The same philosophy is being used at Costco. Any day you go to Costco there will normally be people giving out free samples of their products.

Don't sit there waiting for permission to show the customer different features and benefits of your product or service. If you hesitate at this point and wait for a response, they will decline. The technique for showing a sample or a demonstration is very easy. Don't ask—show. Most of the time if you ask, their answer will be "no." That is an automatic reaction. Many customers don't understand all the features and benefits for many of the products or services offered. Even when you try to explain, some may not believe you. That's why showing or giving a sample is very important. It takes the doubt away and builds trust. Ask questions to make them aware of the different features the product offers. Trying to push customers to invest in the product or service before you educate them, puts pressure on them and they will resist. The more convincing the demonstration is, the more emotional triggers are activated.

The following is an example how to implement the first six steps to close more sales more often:

- Greet with a smile.
- Build rapport.
- Find out the last time the customer had his car detailed or waxed.
- Make him aware of any problems i.e. scratches, oxidation, paint fading, etc.
- Explain the cause of the problem.
- Let him know that this problem should be fixed sometime in the near future to avoid damage to the finish and restore the shine. (Do not try to sell at this time.)
- Ask if he is interested in detailing his car sometime in the **future** (not today) to fix the imperfection, restore the shine and protect the paint.
- "As you can see we have many cars for detail, I don't think we have time to detail your car today."
- "Pull your vehicle to the side. Let me show you a sample. And I'll give you some information in case you decide to have it done sometime in the future."
- As you can see the previous bullet points serve many purposes to motivate the prospect subconsciously to make the right decision today.

Like: You greet with a smile and build rapport

Problem: They are aware of the imperfection of their vehicle (pain).

Educate: When you educate on the cause of the problem, the process of how to fix the damage and how to maintain the vehicle in the future ("Wow" information), you become the expert of your field and the authority on the subject.

Urgency: Can't wait too long or you may risk damaging the paint.

Commitment: A future commitment to detail the car means they realize the current problem and are open to the idea of detailing their vehicle.

Create demand: The fact you have many cars for detail shows there is a need to have detailing done.

Social proof: "Many other people are detailing their vehicles here, they must be a reputable business. If others trust them so can I."

Scarcity: "They are too busy, I hope they have time to detail my car today." It is human behavior starting from childhood. We always want what we can't have.

Solution: Problem can be fixed (pleasure).

Reciprocity: When you give a demonstration and fix an imperfection on the vehicle (or give a free sample), people feel obligated to give back. In this case purchase your service.

It is very important up to this point, not to try to sell detail service, because this will turn on the customer's defense mechanism. Following these simple steps will help you gain the unfair advantage.

- What about your service or product?
- Can you identify a problem, or a potential problem that your service or product can solve for the customer?
- Can you show the demand for your product or service?
- Can you encourage clients to make a fast decision because of the scarcity of your product or service?

8. Trigger emotional senses.

When more of the customer's senses are involved, allow the customer to see, touch, feel, taste or smell the benefits. The more of the customer's senses are involved. the emotional triggers are stronger. At the same time, sell the quality of the product and the reputation of the company.

Knowing that people buy based on what they want, before they buy what they need, your job is to make them want what you are selling. Want is the emotion. For example a prospect needs a car for transportation. Color, make, model, features, wheels, engine, options, are all part of want and emotion. For every need there are at least ten wants.

9. Ask questions.

As a professional, you have to be in control of the conversation. You do that by asking questions and using your senses accordingly. We have two ears and one mouth. We should listen twice as much as we talk. The questions should be structured to keep the customer involved, trigger emotions, get minor agreements, handle objections, lead them to make the right decision to purchase your product or service and close the sale. Some emotional triggers are: pride of ownership, enjoyment of the product or service, peer pressure, status, appearance, first impression and self-image. The reason we ask questions is because, when we tell them something, they doubt it, however, when they verbalize it, they believe it. The questions should be structured to lead them to the conclusions we want them to have.

- **Control by asking questions.**

The average salesperson doesn't realize that by talking too much they can lose their customers' interest if customers feel the salesperson is too pushy. If you talk too much, customers will not hear you; they filter out the noise and stand there out of politeness. When customers feel that the salesperson is too pushy, they build an invisible wall between themselves and the salesperson. What salespeople need to learn is that every sentence they speak has to end with a question mark. If customers ask a question, salespeople have to answer back with a question and lead customers to answer their own question.

When asking questions, customers have no choice but to give full attention because they have to hear the question to give an answer. Make sure the questions you ask lead to the answers you want to hear. Lead them through questions to make them aware of the problem and help them to make the right decision.

> *"You cannot have customers arrive at a decision unless you have already made that decision for them."*

- **Your professional opinion**

It is very important to sell the customer what she really needs, regardless of the cost. What I mean by this, is that it is not up to the salesperson to decide if the price is over the customer's budget or not. It is up to the customer to make that decision. If the customer can't afford the best product, then you should offer the next best product. People buy with emotion and defend their purchase logically. Because they buy what they want, not what they need, they will spend more than they usually do. Lead them with emotional triggers and questions. Don't sell them—educate them. This is how you build trust and friendship, and this is how you get referrals from customers.

- **Ask yes-questions.**

A *yes*-question is a specific set of questions with only one logical answer: "Yes." These types of questions lead customers to realize the present situation and lead to the obvious solutions. All these minor *yes*-answers are minor agreements, which help lead to the final "yes." *Yes*- questions must become a speech habit even in your regular life, and it must become natural. Selling is nothing but minor *yes*-answers that lead to the major decision, which is the final "yes."

- **Answer a question with a question.**

You should always answer a question with another question. Your job is to try to close the sale every time. Take advantage of a customer's question to test close. Always answer the question with a question. This is another example from my carwash business between a customer and an untrained ticket writer:

Customer: "Can you detail the car in two hours?"

Ticket writer: "Yes, we can."

Customer: "That's good to know—I don't have two hours today. Next time."

In this case, the ticket writer already lost the sale. Here is a conversation between a customer and a professional salesperson.

Customer: "Can you detail the car in two hours?"

Salesperson: "You mean, if we can have it done in two hours, you are going to detail it today?" (Notice the word *if*. It gives the impression that "I'm not sure we can.")

Customer: "Yes."

Salesperson: "Let me check." (The salesperson talks to the detailers for a minute then comes back.) "Good news, I have two people who will start on it right now so as not to waste your time, and they will have it ready in one hour and forty-five minutes. Would you rather wait inside or do you want to watch them start the detail?" Notice I did not reconfirm because that

190

shows hesitation and you don't want to reconfirm and re-open the door for the customer to change his mind. The customer already confirmed that, if we could have it ready in two hours, he would have it done today. Think of a tennis player who hits the ball back to the other side of the court every time it comes to him or her. That's exactly like answering a question with a question.

- **Alternative question**

An alternative question is asking the customer a question that has two different answers, but both answers confirm that they are going ahead with the service. Here are some examples:

Salesperson: "Mr. Client, would you want us to just detail the outside or do you want to detail the inside too?"

Salesperson: "What time would you want your car to be ready? At 4:00 or is 5:00 OK?"

Salesperson: "Are you going to need a ride or is someone picking you up?"

Salesperson: "What delivery time is better for you, morning or afternoon?"

The above questions each have two answers. Either answer will confirm they are going ahead with the service.

- **Seek to understand.**

You should always seek to understand before you're understood. This technique is important for two reasons.

- o When a customer brings up a concern, repeat it back to them so they elaborate. Sometimes, when you repeat their question, they come up with their own answer.
- o You should also repeat questions to customers to show that you were listening, and eliminate any confusion and misunderstanding.

Salesperson: "Let me make sure I understand what your concerns are. You want to make sure we remove all these carpet stains, the water spots on the front windshield and those scratches you have on the hood. Are there any other concerns that I missed?"

Customer: "No, that's it."

Salesperson: "Let me make a note of that for the detailer and I will personally check on it."

By them answering the question they have already decided to detail their vehicle.

> *As a salesperson you always want your ears to be open and listening for signs that the customer is willing and ready to go ahead with the sale. Whenever a customer is ready, stop the presentation and close.*

- **Learn from the past.**

Ask qualified questions to learn if the customer has purchased the product or service in the past. Ask proper questions to find out what she liked most about the previous purchase and what she liked least. By doing so, you are not only making sure to pay more attention to these specific areas, but you are also gaining the customer's trust. During your presentation you should assure the customer that the entire product or service will be positive. You should also mention, that what she liked most about the previous service or product, is nothing compared to the features and benefit of this service or product. And what she liked least about the previous widget will not be a problem. Explain why and tell her she will be very happy with the end result. For example, say the customer had his home carpet cleaned and it smelled for three days after it was shampooed. A salesperson should respond in this way:

Salesperson: "The carpet cleaning process, equipment, and chemicals have changed so much in the last three years. We invested thousands of dollars on research to determine the cause and how to tackle the issue. The reason your carpet had a bad smell last time was because it was shampooed using water and soap. Water goes through the carpet and settles on the pad. Then, the next day, it attracts bacteria that not only causes a bad smell, but is also dangerous to your health and the health of your loved ones. Since the research, we invested thousands of dollars on vapor steam cleaning equipment to steam clean carpets instead of shampooing. Not only does it leave your carpet dry and odorless, it also kills any bacteria, and removes stubborn stains that regular shampooing can't. Wait until you see the finished carpet this time."

10. Defuse tension.

As professional salespeople, we never put pressure on customers to make purchasing decisions. We lead them by questions to make the right decision. But sometimes a customer feels pressured and starts building a wall to protect them from the salesperson. If this happens, we have to defuse the tension using the *by-the-way-technique*. For example, "By the way, I see you have golf clubs in the trunk. I golf too. What is your handicap? After the customer relaxes, lead with a question to bring him/her back to sale at hand.

11. Don't make the price the main issue.

We've already mentioned this. It's not about the price; it's about the value. If a salesperson gives the price before explaining the product or service, building value, showing the need, or triggering emotions, then what would the customer have to compare the price to? Obviously the product, at this point, will be too expensive in the customer's opinion and most likely will walk away. If the salesperson makes the price the main issue, then he is facing two problems:

How low can he take the price so the product or service looks cheap enough for the customer to purchase?
The customer may be concerned that the quality is poor because the price is too cheap. "You get what you pay for!"

How should you handle the question if a customer stops you during a presentation to ask about the price of the product or service? A professional salesperson should respond in one of the following manners:

Ignore the question.
"Don't worry about the price now, but let me tell you about the advantage of this widget."
"Are you going to invest in the product right now?"
"I'll make sure you're very happy. Let me finish this first, then I'll show you the investment options."
"We have different options and prices. Let me go over the options first to know which one best suits your needs."

"I'll get to that in a second."

12. Build value.

As illustrated previously, you must build and show the value for every product. The total value price will be much higher than the price you offer the package to the customer. An example would be:

Dinner Special

Salad $8

Appetizer $12

Main Course $25

Dessert $10

Total Value $55

Today's Special $35

Because we itemized each product and gave it a value, the Today's Special for $35 looks like a very good deal. It's a 37 percent discount. Now you have a better chance to promote it and sell it. On the other hand, if you just list the products without the dollar value and only list Today's Special $35, there is no value to compare it to so it sounds expensive.

13. "No" doesn't mean "no."

Twenty years ago the average customer may have said, "No" six times before saying, "Yes." Today, because consumers have became more aware of sales techniques, they say, "No" eight times before saying, "Yes." The first "no" doesn't count; it's a defensive mechanism that we learned when we were kids. Most of the time when customers still say "no" at this point it is because the salesperson did not follow the *recipe*. The recipe is the twelve previous steps above that build rapport, educate, create a need and want, trigger emotions, and build value.

14. Find the last objection, isolate it, and then solve it.

A professional salesperson has a few techniques with which to find the final objection, isolate it, and make sure there are no other objections. When a customer says, "I'll think it over," it's because he has an objection. That's a polite way for customers get rid of salespeople.

- **Columbo technique**

This is also known as the doorknob technique. *Columbo* is a great TV show that ran for over 30 years. Columbo is a police detective who solves crimes. While interrogating a suspect, if he felt the suspect was tensing up, he would use the doorknob technique. He informed the suspect that he was done for now and excuses himself to leave. He would go to the door and hold the doorknob. Meanwhile, the suspect relaxes and drops his guard, thinking he's off the hook. Then Columbo would turn around and say, "I have one more question." Then he will have another chance to try to close again.

- **"I want to think it over."**

After we try everything and the customer says, "I'll think it over," we thank him for his time, let him go and ask him to give it careful consideration. At this time, the customer drops his guard. As he's walking away, the salesperson approaches him and says:

Salesperson: *"Hey John, just to clarify my thinking, may I ask you a question?"*

Customer: *"Yes."*

Salesperson: *"What is it you want to think over? Is it the quality of the service?"*

Customer: *"No."*

Salesperson: *"Is it the time it takes?"*

Customer: *"No."*

Salesperson: *"Is it something I forgot to cover?"*

Customer: *"No, you covered everything."*

Salesperson: *"Be honest with me, is it the money?"*

Customer: *"Yes."*

Salesperson: *"Is there any other reason?"*

Customer: *"No."*

Note: Every time the customer says, "no" to one of these questions, in a sense he is saying, "yes" for the product or service because an objection has been eliminated. We will handle the money objection later in this chapter.

- **One to ten technique**

Salesperson: *"From all the feedback I got from you, I believe you understand that you want and need to invest in this product soon. I'm not asking you to invest in it today but may I ask you a question?"*

Customer: *"Yes."*

Salesperson: *"On a scale from one to ten, one being not at all interested, and ten being you want the product right now, where do you stand?"* (Note: Once the customer is willing to play the number game then most likely they are ready to buy. The closer the number is to ten, the easier it will be to close. If the number is below six that means the salesperson hasn't followed all the above steps.)

Customer: *"Seven."*

Salesperson: *"What would it take to get you to nine or ten?* (After the customer gives you the answer, i.e. price, then ask the following question to isolate the objection.)

Salesperson: *"Is there any other reason?"*

Customer: *"No."*

Whatever reason the client gives you now, you can say. *"You mean I did not explain that to you?"* and you go back to your closing techniques.

- **Money objections**

Common objections include, "I'll think it over, "I don't have time" and the most common is the money objection, "It's too expensive." First, review everything you've already discussed. Go over the work process, the advantage of your service or your product, the quality, the value. Trigger emotion, pain and pleasure. Go over the reason why the customer needs the product or service, the labor time involved, all the minor agreements, get an acknowledgment from the customer that they need the product or service sometime in the near future, then:

Salesperson: *"The price is $300. How much is too much?"*

Customer: *"Can you give it to me for $250?"*

Salesperson: *"That is a big discount, I don't think I can. If I can, I will. What if we split the difference and make it $275?*

(Notice "If I can" means, I'm not sure I can, but what if I can? Get the commitment first from the customer before agreeing.)

Or

Salesperson: *"I wish I could lower the price, but that is our best offer and believe me, I want to earn your business. What if I offer you extra complimentary services worth at least $50?"*

Or

Salesperson: *"Let me check with my manager to see if I can offer it to you for $250. If he says "yes," are you going to do it today?"* (You must get the commitment before you make the offer.)

Customer*: "OK."*

Or

You may offer the customer a combination of discounts plus a free extra service.

What if the customer refuses to give you his final objection, which most likely is the price?

Here's how to handle that situation.

Salesperson*: "What if I give you an offer you can't refuse?"*

Customer: *"What is it?"*

Salesperson: *"If I give you an offer you can't refuse, can we sign the paperwork today?"*

Customer: *"Maybe."*

Salesperson: *"I have to get the offer approved by the manager, and I can't do that unless you commit to the purchase today."*

Customer: *"Okay, I agree."*

Salesperson: *"Let me see if I get it approved by the manager and I'll be right back."*

You then offer to give them a combination of discounts plus some free extra services. Normally, if it is a good deal they will say yes. But what if you offered them the deal and they said:

Customer: *"I'll think about it."*

Salesperson: *"You agree that this is a good offer don't you?"*

Customer: *"Yes."*

Salesperson: *"Then that's not fair. You agreed that if I could get you a great offer you would go ahead with the purchase. I had to beg the manager and assured him you were going to make the purchase today."*

Customer: *"OK, let's do it."*

- **Reduce to the ridiculous.**

Today, most things do cost more. Can you tell me how much is too much?

Find out how much is too much. Find out what the lifetime of the product is.

Divide the "too much" amount by the "life time years" of the product. Divide the annual amount by 365 days. You will now have the daily "too much amount."

Salesperson: "We are only talking about thirty cents a day for you to enjoy the benefits of this widget."

15. Offer incentives and establish a sense of urgency.

Incentives equal value. Around the holidays, department stores offer sales to draw in customers. Everyone likes to save money. Shopping during the holidays has a sense of urgency, because these discounts will not last forever. When you propose to the customer an offer they can't refuse, you have to use the sense of urgency to close. "This offer is available today only. Take advantage of it and save money. You like to save money don't you? Next week this offer will not be available, so take advantage of it today!"

16. Close the sale (Open a relationship).

The average customer is hesitant to make a decision for fear of making the wrong choice. That is why a salesperson leads them through emotional triggers to help them make the right decision. Salespeople should constantly watch and listen for closing signals from customers and be ready to close the sale whenever the customer is ready. Once the customer is ready, there is no reason to continue the presentation. I personally prefer to call it "open a relationship" instead of closing the sale, because this should be the beginning of a great relationship. Besides getting you repeat business, the relationship will be the source of many new clients.

Two telltale signs that the customer is ready for the close:

Body language. Look at their facial expressions. Watch to see how much attention the customer is paying to you and how much he is interested in what you are saying.

Customer asking questions. If a customer is asking a lot of questions, this is a sign that he is very interested and ready to close the sale. When the customer asks a question, the salesperson should try to respond with a test close or a conditional question.

- **Test closing**

Test closing questions are questions that give you feedback on how the customer feels about making a purchasing decision right now. When we talk to customers, we always try to close at any time possible. We always test close. Whenever we feel the customer is ready, a professional salesperson stops the presentation and gives the product to the customer to purchase. No need for more explanation. If the salesperson keeps talking, two things could happen:

Customers realize the salesperson is not listening to him. They are ready to go ahead and purchase the product, but the salesperson is not listening, so they may change their mind.

The longer the salesperson talks, the more likely they will give customers reasons not to go ahead and purchase the product.

When the customer is ready and willing to purchase the product or service, just stop the presentation, give them the product or service, and bring them to the cash register.

- **Conditional closing**

The name says it all. When the customer asks you a question (i.e. "Can I have this product today?") that is a condition. If a customer asks a conditional question (i.e. "Can you include product X with the purchase?"), don't answer the question. Instead, just hand him the product with product X included and lead them to the cash register. No need to confirm. If you do, then you risk the chance that the customer will give you an objection.

Another example is, if the customer says, "Can you give me a $20 discount?" If you can, just give them the product, smile, thank the customer and ask them to go to the cash register to pay for the product. Customers have the right to say "no" when you hand them the product, but they usually don't. The customer gave you a conditional question, so act on it. If you feel more comfortable, you can answer with a confirmation question, such as: "You mean if I can discount the price by $20 you would purchase the product now?"

- **The final question**

As I mentioned before, in 1989, I attended my first sales seminar with Tom Hopkins. I learned the following from him and I have used it since. He said, "When you ask the final question," he paused for few seconds then he screamed as loud as he could and said, "SHUT UP." He paused for few seconds then continued in a low voice, "The first person who talks loses." I have been using this technique since then. Once you ask a closing question, shut up and wait for an answer. The longer the prospect waits to answer, the harder it is to say, "No." Thirty seconds may feel like eternity, but that's okay. The longest I've waited for an answer was about three minutes. This is a very powerful clause. It does not matter how good a job you did in your presentation; if you speak first, you will relieve the pressure from the prospect and it will be easier for him to say, "No."

17. Silence means consent.

The mistake average salespeople make, is that they want to hear the word "yes," and want the customer to reconfirm. That shows hesitation and runs the risk of losing the sale. My point is, sometimes you don't have to hear the word "yes" to go ahead and ring up the sale, as long as you don't hear the word "no." We all learned from our parents that silence means consent. These days, after I ask the final question, I stand silent reading the prospect's body language and wait for the answer. After sixty to ninety seconds of silence, as I am standing in front of the buyer, I look at my salesperson and ask him to ring up the ticket. I have never had a customer ask, "What are you doing?" Customers are normally happy with the decision and go pay for the service.

18. Up-sell using features and benefits.

According to the 80-20 Pareto Principle, 80 percent of your revenue comes from 20 percent of your customers. Any customer has the potential to be that top customer. Therefore, always take advantage of the opportunity and offer upgrades using features and benefits.

The upgrade has to have more value and incentive than the original package. The method to promote this is based on the cost difference of what they already agreed to pay and the price of the new package. For instance, the old package cost $200 and the new package costs $300. So basically, they will get all these extra services that are normally valued at $225 for only $100. Studies show that customers who invest money on a product or service are often willing to spend more on upgrades after closing the original sale.

19. Sell them in bunches like bananas.

When a customer is willing to purchase from you, most likely he is willing to purchase more. Bunch items together that complement each other and sell them as packages. Or package the same items together and sell them in bunches at a discounted price to increase the value and encourage the sale.

20. Gift certificates

Gift certificates are a great source of income. Many times customers do not have time for the service you offer. If you did your job and got them emotionally involved, do not let them leave without asking them to pay for the service and purchase a gift certificate. Offer incentives with the certificate such as purchasing today for an extra discount. The certificate should be 100 percent refundable.

21. Referrals

Ask every customer for a referral. Give incentives to refer family members, friends, and coworkers. Add a referral section on the back of the salesperson's business card. Write the customer's name on the business card. Hand the customer a few business cards and say, "I'm sure many of your friends, family, and coworkers will be commenting on how nice is the new product. Would you do me a favor and hand out my business cards? If you notice, I have your name written on the back so I will know that you referred them. I promise I will take care of them and they will be as pleased as you are right now. For every referral who purchases, I will give you a complimentary $25 credit as appreciation. Would you do that for me?"

22. Follow up

It is a good habit to keep a record of all customers who purchased from you with their name, phone number, and email address; then follow up with them the next day to make sure they are happy with your product or service. If they were happy with the product, now they will be ecstatic because they did not expect you to follow up. If they have questions, then you should be glad you called to help them. If they have a complaint, you have a great opportunity to apologize, and correct the problem.

The follow up is a great way to exceed customer expectation. Now they will definitely refer you to their friends. How many businesses do you know that call customers after purchases to follow up? Calling customers will impress them and make them more loyal. They will brag about the experience to their friends and family members. Use email to keep in touch with your top customers and send them offers at least once a month.

Orphan prospects fall off a company's radar for many different reasons. Maybe a sales rep quits and no one takes over his accounts. Maybe an unprofessional rep fails to follow up with these potential customers. So, look up these records, call the customers and reactivate the relationship. These potential customers could lead to new sales.

23. Testimonial letters

For years, I've been collecting testimonial letters from happy customers to use as third party close and similar situation close. Quotes from customer letters could also be part of your brochures or posted on a sign in the waiting area. Letters from happy customers are good tools to close many sales. These letters should have the customers' names and preferably their phone numbers, and their authorization for potential customers to call them directly if they have questions. I've never had a customer ask to call, but having the permission is a great tool that you will probably never have to use.

The best way to get these letters is to first, ask for them. Then you can offer to write it for them and take it to them to sign, or wait until they visit you next time to have them approve and sign. Ask those happy customers to give you some bullet points on what they want to include in the letter. By writing these letters yourself, you can add the emotional triggers—brag about the quality, talk about the problem and the solution, mention customer concerns before the purchase and their reaction after the purchase. Satisfied customers will be very happy to sign these letters for you.

A third party close is when a customer is doubting the quality or end result and needs an opinion from a third party to help them make the right decision. It also builds trust and triggers emotions.

Similar situation letters are used when a customer has a certain concern and/or objection. Then you say, "Funny you mentioned that! I had a customer with the same concerns, but after he made the purchase he wrote me this letter."

Note: These days you may take a video testimonial on your smart phone and have it readily available whenever you need to use it.

CHAPTER 21

59 Tactical Training Questions

Questions to Open the Door for the Sale

1. **How would you like...**

   ...To make your electric bill disappear?

   ...to enhance your pride of ownership?

   ...to be the envy of all your friends?

   ...to make your car look like a showroom car right out of the dealer's lot?

   ...to lose fifty pounds in six months?

   ...to feel more energetic every morning?

   ...to get rid of your emotional upset right now?

   ...to learn how to increase profits in the next 20 minutes?

   ...to increase the value of your car?

   ...to sell your house faster?

   ...to say "Wow" every time you enter your house?

   ...to reduce your allergy and asthma problems?

2. **May I tell you about a service we provide that will...**

   ...enhance your pride of ownership?

   ...make you the envy of all your friends?

   ...make you feel younger again?

   ...make you feel happy again?

   ...make you sell your house faster?

   ...helps you lose weight?

   ...improve your financial status?

   ...make you say "Wow" every time you enter your house?

3. **Would you be interested in a service we provide that can...**

    ...make you enjoy driving your car all over again?

    ...enhance your pride of ownership?

    ...make you the envy of all your friends?

    ...help you lose weight?

    ...help sell your house faster?

    ...get rid of your emotional upset?

    ...reduce your allergy and asthma problems?

4. **Would you be interested in learning about a special we are offering to a few of our customers that can...**

    ...increase the value of your vehicle?

    ...enhance your pride of ownership?

    ...make you the envy of all your friends?

    ...help you lose fifty pounds in six months?

    ...help you feel more energetic every morning?

    ...help sell your house faster?

5. **For people in your position, image, perception and impressions are very important. Can I show you how we can help you to...**

    ...be the envy of your friends and associates?

    ...increase profit 30 percent in thirty days?

    ...enhance your pride of ownership?

    ...make your car look like a brand new car right out of the dealer's lot?

    ...make your car shine ten times brighter?

6. **Would you like to learn about a non-surgical procedure (said with a smile) that can...**

    ...get rid of your emotional upset right now?

    ...help you lose weight fast?

    ...make you feel more energetic every morning?

    ...eliminate the cause of your allergy and asthma symptoms?

7. **Questions you can ask to help sell memberships.**

...If there were an option to keep your home protected for less than $10 a week, would you be interested?

...Would you be interested in a membership club that can save you 63 percent off your expenses?

...May I show you a way of slashing your expenses by over 63 percent and at the same time keep your car in tip-top shape?

8. **Would you like to know about a breakthrough in technology/products/service that can...**

...make you feel more energetic?

...help you lose weight faster?

...increase the value of your vehicle?

...help you sell your home faster?

...eliminate the cause of your allergy and asthma symptoms?

9. **May I show you a service we provide that has been voted #1 by XYZ two years in a row that can...**

...make you enjoy driving your car all over again?

...enhance your pride of ownership?

...make you the envy of all your friends?

...help you lose twenty pounds in twenty days?

...increase profit 30 percent in thirty days?

...increase the value of your service?

...help you sell your home faster?

10. **Are you interested in owning the...**

...most beautiful home in your neighborhood?

...the shiniest car in your neighborhood?

...the cleanest and greenest yard in your neighborhood?

11. **Does increasing the value of your home by thousands of dollars interest you?**

12. **Is being able to sell your home fast at the highest price possible important to you?**

13. **I see you are a professional (i.e., real estate). Since your car's appearance could be important to your business, wouldn't you like to learn how to...**

    ...enhance your professional image with a nicer-looking car?

    ...make the clients who ride with you feel more comfortable?

    ...make your car look like a brand new car right out of the dealer's lot?

    ...remove these scratches right now?

    ...remove the stains on your carpet?

14. **Would you like to save money on your ...**

    ...purchase?

    ...investment?

    ...future investment?

15. **I assume you wouldn't mind having ...**

    ...a free lunch on us?

    ...this service if it were offered to you right now for free?

16. **Have you heard about...**

    ...our risk-free money-back guarantee offer?

    ...our special that we're running today?

    ...our radio special?

17. **Are you here for the...**

    ...special we're running?

    ...VIP program?

    ... membership program?

18. **Are you a VIP member?**

19. **Have you seen our VIP brochure? Would you like to see how much money you can save by joining?**

20. **What would be more important to you—to eliminate these problems or to save money? (Wait for answer.) Well, I have good news for you—I can offer you both. Would you like to know how?**

21. **May I ask you a question?**

    ...When was the last time you had this service done?

    ...Would you like to stay in tip-top shape?

    ...Would you like to save money?

    ...Would you like to remove f these stains?

Rapport Builders

22. **Find a common interest, such as friends or anything else you might have in common with your client. People trust people who have something in common with them. It is imperative to always tell the truth.**

    ...Welcome back.

    ...Are these your children?

    ...They are great-looking kids!

    ...How old are they?

    ...I have kids, too. They're about the same age as your kids.

    ...Aren't they great?

    ...What school do they go to/what grade are they in?

    ...Are you going to watch (did you watch)...

        The football/basketball/baseball game?

        What's your favorite team?

        The boxing match?

    ...I'm really impressed with your vehicle...

        You really take care of it.

        It's a very nice color.

        I love the power.

        I love those features in it.

My wife drives one of these.

It's a very safe car.

Have you seen the 20/20 report about these cars?

What is it you like most about your car?

...That is an interesting book in your hand. I've read it.

...It's a beautiful day today, isn't it?

...Isn't it good not to have rain for a few days?

...Are these your golf clubs? Oh, I love golfing too.

What is your handicap?

How often do you golf?

...That's a nice tie you have on.

...I'm sorry for the wait. I was taking care of that customer. Now I'm all yours.

...Did you hear what just happened? It's all over the news.

...What company do you work for? (Wait for answer.) Do you know (insert name)?

...What is your field of business? (Wait for answer.) (insert name) is my good friend do you know him?

Conditional Close

23. **Find out if the customer is ready to commit to the sale after you solve the objection and explain all the values and advantages**.

    ...If I can save you a lot of money today, would there be any reason not to go ahead with the service today?

    ...If I can give it to you at the price you're asking, ...

    Could we go ahead and approve the agreement today?

    Would you want us to deliver today or tomorrow?

    ...If I make you an irresistible offer that can save you a lot of money, would you start the service right now? (Customer must agree, "yes" before you present your offer.)

    Would you want us to deliver today?

    ...If we can remove these stains, are you planning on having the service done today?

...If I can give you a ride, would you leave your car today?

...If we call your spouse and explain the program and he/she thinks it's good, could we go ahead with the service today?

...If we can start on it right now and be done in two hours, would you have it done today?

...Are you planning on detailing your car today or sometime next week?

...Suppose I can lower the price by 10 percent, would that help you make up your mind to start the service today?

...Suppose we can get around the price problem. Is that the only reason stopping you from making the right decision?

...If we can have it done by four o'clock today, do you want us to start on it right now?

Test Close or Minor Agreement Close

24. **These are questions you ask before the customers agree to the service but by answering they have already committed to the service. The only way they can answer these questions is if they already visualized that they agreed to go ahead.**

    * How much time do you have allotted for this service?
    * What time and day do you want us to deliver?
    * Do you want to take the warranty with you now or when you pick up the product?
    * Are you going to surprise your spouse with this gift?
    * Will you need a ride or will someone pick you up?
    * Do you want us to pick you up when the car is ready or do you have a ride?
    * What are your expectations from this service?
    * How do you imagine the widget will look after we're done?
    * How will you be paying: cash or credit?
    * What type of warranty would you prefer: X or Y?
    * Which price range best fits your budget?
    * What kind of price did you have in mind?
    * If price were not an issue, which one would you prefer?

25. **I don't know how you feel, but...**

    ...aren't you tired of all those stains?

    ...aren't you tired of paying these bills?

...aren't you tired of the high interest?

26. **Suppose that we have another package that gives you all these benefits at 20 percent less, would you be interested? (Wait for answer.) You're in luck today! We have this package on sale at 30 percent of the cost. That solves that, doesn't it? Let's fill out the paperwork.**

27. **Suppose we have a service that can _____, would you give me 20 minutes of your time to**

    ...enhance your pride of ownership

    ...remove all these stains

    ...restore the shine of the paint

    ...make you the envy of all your friends

28. **Let me ask you...**

    ...what can we do to earn your business today?

    ...what's keeping you from making up your mind now?

    ...would you like to save money?

    ...on a scale of 1 to 10, how do you rank our quality?

    ...on scale 1 to 10, how likely are you to invest in the product today?

29. **If we can meet your needs, do we have an agreement?**

30. **Are you interested in saving $800 a year on this service?**

31. **Would you agree that the quality of a product is remembered much longer than the price?**

32. **Would you agree you get what you pay for?**

33. **Would you agree that quality and service are more important?**

34. **Would you agree the safety of your family is more important than a few extra dollars?**

Customers' Expectations

35. **Objective: To exceed customers' expectations.**

    ...If I had a magic wand and I could give you the finished product that you want, what would it be like?

    ...Tell me, what are your major concerns?

    ...The last time you had your car detailed, what did you like most about the detail?

    ...The last time you had your car detailed, what did you like least about the detail?

    ...What are your expectations from the service?

    ...What do we have to do to make you completely happy?

    ...Could you tell me the three major concerns you have?

Seek to Understand

36. **To understand exactly what your customer's expectations are.**

    You mentioned that you are interested in _____. What do you mean by that?

    ...higher quality

    ...a longer-lasting finish

    ...removing certain stains

    You expressed an interest in _____. What exactly are you looking for?
    ...leather protection

    ...fabric protection

    You said that a guarantee is important. What do you consider a strong guarantee?

    How soon do you want it to be delivered?

    When you said _____, what did you mean by it?

    What exactly did you mean when you said _____?

    Let me make sure I understand. You said _____, is that it?

Feedback

37. Repeat all the features and benefits to customers

Now that I have explained to you about XYZ...

    ...can you see how it can protect your loved ones?

    ...can you see how it can save you a lot of money?

    ...do you understand how it works?

    ...can you see that quality, service and reputation are important to us, and we'll do whatever needs to be done to exceed your expectations?

    ...do you understand our detail process and the extra stages and steps we take to ensure the highest quality service? Do you feel more at ease?

    ...I sense that you liked those benefits and features. Is there something else you need or still want to know about?

    ...You seem pleased with these benefits and features. Are you?

    ...Are you comfortable with the guarantee?

    ...Do you see the advantage of having your house...

        protected?

        cleaned?

        painted?

    ...Is it important for you to have this...

        guarantee?

        stain removed?

        scratch removed?

    ...Now that I have explained to you all the benefits, which two are the most important to you?

    ...What would your spouse think of this...

        warranty?

    ...removal of bacteria and dust mites from interior fabrics?

    ...Am I correct to assume these are the features you had in mind?

    ...Would you mind telling me if there is any other feature or benefit you are still looking for that I didn't mention?

    ...Do these features meet your expectations?

    ...Can you see the savings for joining the VIP program?

...I have been doing all the talking. Thank you for giving me your undivided attention. May I ask you for your opinion on this program?

Handling Objections

You cannot close the sale until you:

* Find the objection.
* Isolate the objection.
* Handle the objection.

38. **Finding the Objection**

...What's holding you back from deciding today? Is it the quality of the product? Is it the service rendered? Is it our guarantee? Is it the time? Be honest with me, is it the money? (After every question wait for the answer. Most of the time it is the money.)

...Could you help me out, please? I really tried my best to explain to you the advantage of our product, and obviously it wasn't good enough. Could you please help me by telling me what I did wrong or maybe what I need to do to improve? Most people will say, "No, it's not you, you're great." Then you answer, "Then be honest with me, is it the money?"

...Obviously price and quality are important to you. Is there anything else that outweighs these two?

...Your time is valuable. Don't spend $5 of your time thinking about this small decision. By the way, what is it you want to think about? Is it the quality? Be honest with me, is it the money?

...One to ten technique: From all the feedback I got from you, I believe you understand the importance of this service. May I ask you a question? On a scale of one to ten, one being not interested at all, and ten being you want the service right now, where do you stand? (Note: once the customer is willing to play the number game, then most likely they will buy. The closer the number to ten the easier it is to close. If the number is below six, that means the salesperson hasn't followed all the above steps.) Wait for the answer then say, "What does it take to move you up closer to ten?"

39. **Isolate the Objection**

* Is that the only reason?
* Other than this, is there any other reason you can think of?

* Suppose we can solve this problem for you today, is there anything else that's holding you back?
* If this problem did not exist, would you invest today?
* Is this the only issue that's holding you back?
* If we can solve this concern, would you take it home with you now?
* Is this the only concern you have?
* What other concerns do you have?
* I'm glad you brought it up. Is there any other concern?
* Besides this, what other concerns do you have?
* Is there anything else besides...?
* Is it safe to assume that this is your only concern?

40. Handling the Price Objection

* Never sacrifice the truth in order to make a sale; otherwise, you will risk losing business and credibility:
* Yes, our price could be a little higher than other places, but so is our quality. Aren't you interested in longer protection, guarantee, and safety?
* I'd rather apologize one time for the price than a lifetime for the quality. Don't you feel that way, too?
* Yes, the price is a little high, but if you add up all the free services you're receiving, you'll see that it is a great value, isn't it?
* Price too high? Compared to what?
* Price too high? How much is too much?
* If you add up all these free services you'll see they are valued at two times more than the widget is worth alone. Do you agree?
* Most people, when they go shopping, look for the best price, quality, and service. Don't you feel the same way? (Wait for answer.) Isn't it true that when you find the best price it's not the best quality or service? So which is more important to you, the price or the quality and service?
* Sure it costs a little more. However, it will cost much less over the year. Don't you agree?
* Sure, it costs a little more. However, you get three times your money's worth in quality and free services. Don't you agree?
* Wouldn't you agree that the quality of the service is remembered much longer than the price?
* Wouldn't you agree that the sweetness of low price is quickly forgotten when you have to deal with the bitterness of low quality?
* That brings up a question: Is low price more important than the quality and the guarantee?

216

* That brings up a question: Which would be more important to you saving a few dollars with a lower price today or saving hundreds of dollars over the next year?
* That brings up a question: Which would be more important to you saving a few dollars on a lower price today or the safety of your family?
* I understand how you feel about the price, but would you tell me how you feel about our quality?
* I appreciate how you feel about the price. Many of our customers felt the same way at first. However, after the service was rendered, I received hundreds of thank-you phone calls and a lot of letters. Would you like to read some of them now?
* I personally feel the price is too low for what you're getting. Did you add up the value of all the price savings and benefits you'll receive?
* It may look expensive, but don't you think...
* ...it's cheaper than buying a new car?
* ...it's cheaper than a new paint job?
* ...if I could lower the price I would?
* It's $120 more than what you wanted to pay? That's $10 per month or 33 cents per day. Doesn't your car deserve 33 cents a day for all this extra protection it'll receive?
* You want a $20 discount? How about if I give you $40 extra in free services instead, would that be okay with you?
* You want a $____ discount? If I can give it to you at this price you want us to deliver today?
* You found it cheaper down the street? And did they give you all the added perks and guarantee with it? If you weren't satisfied? Did they give you a 30-day wash pass with it?
* This is the lowest price that we can offer this service with all these extra values. If we cut down our price, what quality or service should we cut down as well to still make a profit?
* If I can get you a better price, would you agree?
* As I said at the beginning, this service is not for everyone, it may not be for you. We have other options with lower prices, would you like me to show them to you? They don't include a lot of the benefits I've already mentioned to you.
* We can cut down some of the services and then cut down the price. Is this what you want?
* I can give you a better price if you invest in two products.
* If our competitor's price is lower, what does that tell you?
* Have you ever figured out the price of not investing in a high quality product with a guarantee?

* Don't be deceived by the price. You actually pay less because we give you more: more quality service, more guarantee, more expertise, more security. Isn't that what you're really interested in?
* Aren't you really interested in getting the best value for your dollar? I'll explain all the extra values and benefits you're receiving.
* You're driving a very nice quality car. You are obviously a person who appreciates quality. Why are you denying yourself quality now?
* Why do you think our competition is cheaper? They are in business to make money aren't they? Where do you think they cut corners? Did they cut back on quality and guarantee? You have to worry about where they cut corners. Why not invest with a risk-free, money back guarantee, and sleep better at night?
* We don't do things the cheap way. We believe in quality and a lot of added value that our competition doesn't give you.
* What neighborhood do you live in? You didn't cut corners when buying your house in a good neighborhood. Why cut corners when you are protecting your family?
* The price I gave you already includes a 30 percent discount.

Handling Specific Objections

41. **"I'll think about it."**

* Okay, I'll see you next week. (Wait until the customer is walking away, then...) May I ask you a question? Just to clarify my thinking, what is it that you really want to think about, is it the quality of our service? (Wait for answer) (Every "no" answer confirms that they are buying) Is it the time it takes? Is it something I forgot? Be honest with me, is it the money?
* Obviously you must have a reason for saying that. May I ask what is it?
* I understand you want to think about it. I'm interested in your thoughts about the reason for and against buying now. Would you share them with me?
* Obviously there is something that I didn't explain properly that you want to think over. Would you mind sharing it with me?
* I know what you're saying. You're saying I didn't explain the benefits of the product clearly to you. I apologize for that. Now what didn't I make clear to you?

42. "I don't have a ride."

...You mean if you had a ride you would you leave your car today? Then let me see if someone can give you a ride.

43. "I'll do it next week."

*   Great. What day works best for you so we can fit you in?
*   If I can show you a way to save a lot of money would you pay for it today? We will give you a fully refundable gift certificate that you may redeem at any time.
*   We have a special going today that will not be here next week. Why not take advantage of it? You can also purchase a gift certificate and bring it back later.
*   By pre-paying for it today you can save 20 percent. You like to save money don't you?

44. "I don't have time."

*   Obviously you have somewhere important to go. Are you going to work? How long will you be there? If we were able to give you a ride to work and have the car delivered to you at (specific time), would you be interested?
*   But you like to save money, don't you? Are you planning on detailing the car any time in the near future? Why not take advantage of our gift certificate today to lock down the special price we offered with all these added benefits? And your wash today will be free. The gift certificate is fully refundable.
*   We have a special deal with a rental car agency. We'll give you 30 days of free carwashes valued at $80 if you pay the $16 for a day's car rental and leave your car here for detailing.
*   Okay, are you going to be driving in the area? Where are you going? Are you going to be there for a couple of hours? If I can find someone to give you a ride and have your car ready in less than two hours, then pick you up again, would that be okay with you?
*   When do you ever have time for yourself? Sometimes we have to reward ourselves for working so hard, don't you agree? What's your plan for today? Great. If we could get someone to give you a ride and pick you up again later when your car is ready, does that sound good to you?

45. **"I don't have the money this week." or "I get paid on Friday." or "I don't have any money on me."**

Give them an incentive to make a decision today.
* If you had money, would you do it today?
* How about if we hold your check until Friday?
* You don't have to pay now; you can pay when the job is done. Is that okay?
* We also accept all major credit cards.
* If we can find a way to detail your car today and have you pay later, would you do it?
* We can put it on your credit card and you don't have to pay for thirty days.
* You can pay half with cash, half with a credit card.

46. **"I need to ask my spouse."**

Agree with the customer first, and then find a solution.
* I don't blame you. I would do the same. Tell you what. You agree that what I offered you is a great opportunity and a money savings, isn't it? And you would like to take advantage of it, wouldn't you? Would you like to lock that price down with all these benefits? We can do that if you purchase a gift certificate and put it on your credit card. Then discuss it with your spouse. If he/she doesn't agree, the gift certificate is fully refundable and we credit your credit card.
* Let me ask you, do you have an anniversary or birthday coming up? If so, great. This will make a great gift, don't you agree? We offer gift certificates. If not, ask, "When was the last time you surprised your spouse for no reason, just to say 'I love you?'" We offer "I love you" gift certificates.
* Do you think your spouse will say "yes" or "no"? (Most likely the answer would be "yes.") Where is he/she now? Would you like to use my phone to call him/her? If they say "no..." say, "The reason I asked you to call him/her was because if there are any questions, I could answer them.

47. **"The dealer said not to wax my car."**

...This is a valid concern. As a matter of fact, we have some customers who brought up the same concern before, but after we had their cars detailed, they wrote thanking us. Let me show you some of their letters.

...When you go to the beach and expose your skin to the sun, do you put any protective lotion on it to prevent your skin from burning? Your car needs protection from the burning sun and the elements to prevent it from oxidation.

...Do me a favor. Could you please touch the paint of your car? Do you feel how rough it is? Now touch the paint on this car that we just detailed. Do you feel how smooth it is? Do you see all these black dots on your paint? Do you see all these light scratches on it, versus this other car we just detailed? It doesn't have any because we eliminated them. Do you see the wet-look shine on this car versus yours? Now tell me, do you think that the salesperson at the dealership is right?

...May I show you this manual for Cadillac that recommends having your car waxed every so often? If Cadillac recommends it, don't you think your car also needs it today?

If you shouldn't wax or detail a new car, why is the dealer sending us brand new cars to detail?

...We offer a risk-free money back guarantee. If you don't see a major improvement in the appearance of your vehicle, you don't pay for it. Is that a deal?

48. **"I have this small dent. I need to fix it first."**

...On what would you base your decision today? Is it on this small dent or on the overall appearance of your vehicle?

...You know, in order to have your paint matched you should have your car detailed so they can match to the real color of your car.

...When you have the fender fixed, the car will look funny because the fender will look newer than the rest of the car.

Closing Questions

The answer will confirm that they are going ahead with the sale.

49. **Alternative of choice close**

   * Do you need a ride or will someone be picking you up?
   * Are you interested in the one-year or two-year warranty?
   * Do you want us to call you when the product is ready or will you call us in a few hours?
   * Do you prefer cash or credit?
   * Do you want the added protection with it?
   * What is the best time for you to deliver the product? Morning or afternoon?
   * Do you prefer it in red or blue?

* Are you going to wait for the car, or do you need a ride somewhere?

50. **Assumptive Close**

* I assume that this is what you want, isn't it? Then let's go ahead and begin.
* Could you please fill out this paperwork so we can get started?
* While you're filling out the paperwork, I'll setup delivery.
* I'll call someone to give you a ride right now.
* Let's go over your car to check for any damage before we start the job.
* I assume you want us to begin right away.
* Let me print out a ticket for you to take to the register. Here is your ticket.
* We have one car ahead of yours. We'll be starting on yours within fifteen minutes.
* Okay, let me call someone to set up the work order.
* Would you please print your name here so we can get started?
* Let me give you your receipt.

51. **Incentive Closes**

...This special promotion is only for today. Why don't you take advantage of it? You like to save money, don't you?
...Isn't that a great savings? That savings is for today only.

Shall we go ahead?

You like to save money, don't you? That settles it then, doesn't it?

...The maintenance program we included for you free of charge is a great value, don't you agree? ...Shall we go ahead and add it?
...The added value is worth $200 and that's all free today... Shall we go ahead and add it?
...With the risk-free, money back guarantee, you have nothing to lose and everything to gain, don't you agree?
...If I can get you an extra 10 percent discount, would you agree to invest?
...If I can save you a lot of money today, would you say yes?

52. **Final Close**

* It's settled then. Could you fill out this information?
* Do we have an agreement?
* Should we start on it right away?
* You will be very pleased when your car is ready.
* Let me give you your ticket before we start.

* Fill this paperwork out to begin.
* Let me call someone to start on your car right away.

Minor "yes" Closes. Every minor "yes," contributes to the final major "yes." The only answer they can give you is a "yes."

53. **Scenario 1:**

* Would you like the free guarantee added to the product?
* Would you like the free maintenance service in six months?
* Then should we go ahead and start?

54. **Scenario 2:**

* Do you like the quality? Yes.
* Do you like our warranty plan? Yes.
* Do you like the savings you're receiving? Yes.

Then could you please fill this out so we can begin?

55. **Scenario 3:**

* Does this package best meet your needs? Yes.
* Do you need a ride? Yes.
* You said you're paying cash, aren't you? Yes.

Up-selling Questions

56. **Once a prospect invests in your product or service, it is easy to upgrade them to a better package, as long as it includes better value, features, and benefits.**

* What else do you need?
* If you want the interior done at the same time, you can get a discount. Are you interested?
* If it were more affordable, would you go for this package instead?
* What other needs do you have?
* Did anyone explain to you about the warranty we offer with this service?
* This widget offers a better protection and better quality, and it is a better value as well.
* For $100 more you receive this $300 value. It's like a 70 percent discount. Should we add it to the order?
* How about adding this widget and receiving a 50 percent discount?
* Why not go with the two-year warranty? It's only $150 more.

* We have different options with different prices. Let me explain to you about our best package first. If it's not for you, then I'll tell you about the next best package. Is that okay?

Sell Them in Bunches

57. **Once they've trusted you and made a decision to invest in your service or product, offer them to purchase in bunches like bananas and save money. Think of Costco.**

   ...By the way, if you're planning on detailing your other car you can get an extra 20 percent discount for the second one if you pay for both right now. Is that of interest to you?

   ...Why not detail both cars and receive a 10 percent discount on the total price?

   ...Do you like to save money? You can receive an extra 10 percent discount if you decide to detail both cars today.

   ...If you bring your second car for detail within ten days you'll receive an extra 20 percent discount.

   ...If you purchase a gift certificate for your second car today, you'll get an additional 20 percent discount, shall we add it?

   ...We can give you a big discount if you want to detail two cars. Pay for both today and bring the second car in anytime you want.

Referral Questions

58. **The number one source of new customers is referrals. What are you actively doing to get new business in your doors?**

   * Of your closest friends, who do you think would be most interested in having the same service done?
   * I was wondering if you could help me. Could you give this coupon to two of your colleagues?
   * Who else do you think would be interested in getting the same service?
   * Could you think of two close friends who would enjoy the benefit of this service?
   * Would you take some coupons with you to work and give them to all your friends?

Telephone Follow-Up

59. Most clients do not expect a call after a sale. The phone call is designed to insure that you exceeded their expectations and to get referrals.

Hi, my name is _____. I'm calling from _____. We are calling to follow up and to make sure everything was satisfactory with your service. Do you have a minute?

    ...How do you rate the job on a scale of one to ten?

    ...Is there anything we can do to improve?

    ...Would you recommend us to a friend?

    ...As a valued client, you'll receive an extra 10 percent discount on your next investment within seven days.

    ...If the customer is unhappy...

    ...The reason we called is to make sure you are 100 percent satisfied. If you're not, we are not. When can you come back to fix the issue, Tuesday or Wednesday?

SECTION VII

THE ENTREPRENEUR PRINCIPLE

CHAPTER 22

The Funnel

Increasing customer base, frequency of visits and dollar per transaction are an ongoing process and may require a planned blueprint, time invested to put the plan to work, and a commitment to follow the blueprint steps. Until I attended a live educational session, I had not realized how vital it is to implement a plan of action. Sometimes, it is best to start the plan with the end in mind.

The Funnel Dissected

Advertising media

You may have a most important message that everyone should know about, but if you don't have the vehicle to spread the word and reach your audience, it will be the best-kept secret. There are many vehicles to get your message out. The message will not get out without some sort of investment. The investment is not necessarily money.

Radio Many radio stations may agree on a 50/50 trade if you have something worth trading. The reason is that they have allotted a certain amount of time for advertisements in every hour, and if they don't fill those spots with ads they lose them and cannot get them back up. If you have some good information that the radio station believes its audience would be interested in, you might arrange for a free interview, where you share the "Wow" information and direct the audience to either call or go to your website or squeeze page and leave their email address so you can forward the information to them for free. Radio ads with a call to action, have an immediate response time and it may require you to have a phone system that can handle the calls.

Television These ads are also reasonable if you advertise on cable channels, late at night, or local channels with sponsored advertisements of ten to fifteen seconds. If you are offering newsworthy information to the public, hire a public relation person to contact a local TV station on your behalf to arrange a televised interview on the subject. Direct viewers to your website to register to receive valuable information for free. Half-hour infomercials on local network television stations are very reasonably priced if you reserve a late nightspot. With a good offer the infomercials normally have high response rates.

Billboards Billboards have a good capture rate and are very effective in getting your message out to commuters. Many commuters either tune out commercials or listen to audio books or music CDs instead of the radio; therefore billboards are good vehicle to get your message to them.

Direct mail The advantage of direct mail is that you can pick and choose your area to promote to. The drawback is unless you can barter direct mail advertisement; you need some up front investment.

Flyers Flyers are a very economical way to spread your message. You may print flyers and distribute to high traffic businesses, i.e. offices with many employees and management personnel. The advantage is that it doesn't cost much. The disadvantage is that it is time consuming. Time limits how much you can spread your message, and it is dependent on businesses allowing you to leave your flyers.

Door hangers This is a very effective venue, especially for real estate agents. It is economical. However, it is time consuming unless you hire labor at a minimum wage to do the job for you. (You must ring the bell or knock on the door every time you leave a flyer on the doorknob.) It also limits your exposure on how much you can spread the message.

Newspapers Newspapers may be used as target marketing by adding an insert to a specific area or an ad in the main section to spread the word to the whole city. It may be pricey depending on how big of an ad. All advertising media,, newspaper ads have a low capture rate if only used once or twice; however increasing the frequency of ads, increases the capture rate. You may have to commit to advertising consistently for a month for good results.

Joint ventures Joint ventures are a great way to promote. You make a deal with local businesses that target the same consumers you are trying to target. You supply the product or service and the other party supplies the buyers; then you both share the profit based on a previously signed agreement. Many entrepreneurs use the joint venture strategy with local and national TV and radio stations. This strategy requires no investment up front, and gives access to a qualified list that has been tested and used. Most of all, the prospects already trust and buy from your joint venture partner and will be more receptive to listening to your message.

Social Media was used in President Obama's first and second elections. Many credit a big part of why he won his first election to social media. Start a social media page. Join as many groups as possible with the audience you are looking for. Ask them to join your group. Start an event. Spread your message to the groups you've joined by writing something on their walls. Do not spam and do not sell when you write on someone's wall; just provide information and news to peak their curiosity and have them join your event.

Internet ads are a great way to advertise and promote your business, and may be filtered to target a specific audience. Two main social media ads are: pay per click and banner ads. When you pay per click, your ad will be filtered to target your viewing audience on whatever site they are on and you only pay for results. You pay only if they click on your link to get more information. The banner ads are great for having your message out for a certain period of time on specific websites for all visitors to see.

Blogs are a must. If you don't have a blog start one. Add a blog to your website, create a separate one, or do both. Your blog has to be filled with interesting and useful information about the subject you are trying to promote. Become an active blogger; add new information on a regular basis. It must become a source of valuable and accurate information for all of your followers. Give them incentives to leave their email addresses, such as a free newsletter. A great way to promote your blog is by joining other blogs, add comments and refer to the valuable information on your blog.

Websites and squeeze pages give your message credibility. Have it done and maintained by a professional company that will also promote your page in search engines. Add pictures and video clips and testimonials. Make sure to add these video clips on YouTube as well. Add a blog section and an "Enter Your Email" box. The "Enter Your Email" box has to be located on the landing page. Most people would rather not give you anything for free. What are you going to give first for them to opt-in?

Rent email lists work the same as joint ventures. The only difference is you are not sharing the profit of any sales. The email lists, which are normally collected by local businesses, are active and about 25 percent of your messages will be opened and read. This type of promotion has a one hundred fold, or better, capture rate if you compare to print ads.

Important points in your advertisement message

A capture line, a UVP or USP to grab their attention so they will listen or read.
A sense of urgency to act immediately.
Choose the right media and how to contact you. Most people listen to the radio in their car. If you ask them to go to a website URL to register, your capture rate will be very low. For radio listeners give them an easy to remember phone number. For TV and web surfers direct them to a URL link to register.
Your goal is to collect email addresses, names and maybe cell numbers for text messages.
Once you collect email addresses, you should email them at least once or twice a month with some valuable information to make their reaction be, "Wow, I did not know that."
Hire a Search Engine Optimizer to promote your websites.

> *"Hire people who play at what you work hard at."*

The funnel steps

The funnel blueprint has six steps. You may eliminate two or three steps from the funnel or you may even take prospects straight to the bottom of you funnel if they are ready. The idea behind the funnel metaphor is to collect as many emails as possible, then to move your prospect down the funnel until you have your dream clients. Every step of the funnel requires a bigger commitment from the interested prospect and also requires more "Wow" information from you regarding your service or product. The registered emails will include very hot, hot, warm, room temperature, cold and freezing prospects. They are all interested in your message, but they are at different stages of readiness and motivation to act. If they were not interested in what you have to say, they would not have opted-in to your email database.

The six stages of the funnel

A Free offer. This must be filled with "Wow" information, service or product. It must have a lot of added value in it that will benefit the subscribers of your email list. This is the first and the most important step of the process, and it is worth repeating one more time. If your offer is not free and is not filled with "Wow" information that is worth hundreds of dollars, the funnel plan will not work. If you are not willing to *give before you receive*, why should others pay you and trust you if they don't know you? Give and you shall receive is the law of the universe.

A low offer. The second step of the funnel process. If you gave them a good value with your free offer, many of your prospects will be willing to pay a small premium to get more information, service or product from you. They saw the benefit and value of your first offer, now they trust you to deliver even more value. Many will invest in your low offer just as a thank you for the first free service, product or information you provided to them.

A medium offer. The third step of the funnel. If prospects are willing to pay you money, they are willing to pay you more money for your service and helpful information, as long as you keep increasing the value of what they receive. This step is designed to have your prospect get used to the idea of paying you more money for your product or service.

A medium high offer. The fourth step of the funnel. Raise the stakes on what you are giving the prospect, and charge more money. What you are doing is offering more expensive services or information to the prospect that has the money and is willing to invest in your ultimate product.

A high offer. The last step before your final dream offer that will filter the few elite who will most likely invest in your ultimate business plan.

Your ultimate goal offer. This is why you started this journey. This last step will pay you more than the above five steps combined. The seeds you planted and nourished are now blossoming.

Note: every step of the funnel may have many offers or many programs for the same price. Many of your prospects cannot afford to go to the next step of the funnel. Instead, they may be comfortable investing in more services at the same price they invested previously. For example, you may have five different webinars each covering one principle or one area of the big picture. Promote one seminar at a time for the same prospects.

> *"If you fail to plan, you are planning to fail."*

THE FUNNEL DIAGRAM

Radio, TV, Billboards, Direct Mail, Flyers, Door Hangers, Newspaper, Joint Ventures, Social Media Internet Ads Blogs

Website   Email lists

Free Offer

Low Offer

Medium Offer

Medium High

High

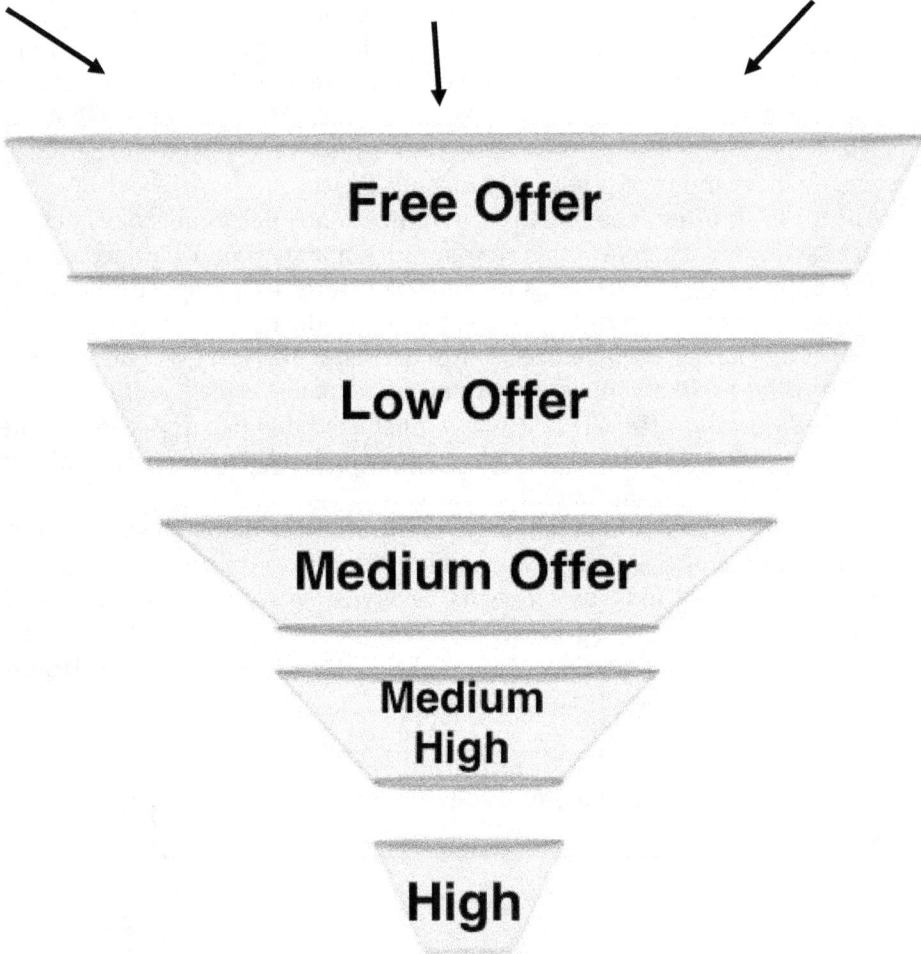

Your Ultimate Goal

For example, what if your ultimate goal is to consult and get paid at least $100,000 for your consulting fee? The plan will be as follows:

Radio, TV, Billboard, Flyers, Email, Social Media, News Paper, Print Ads

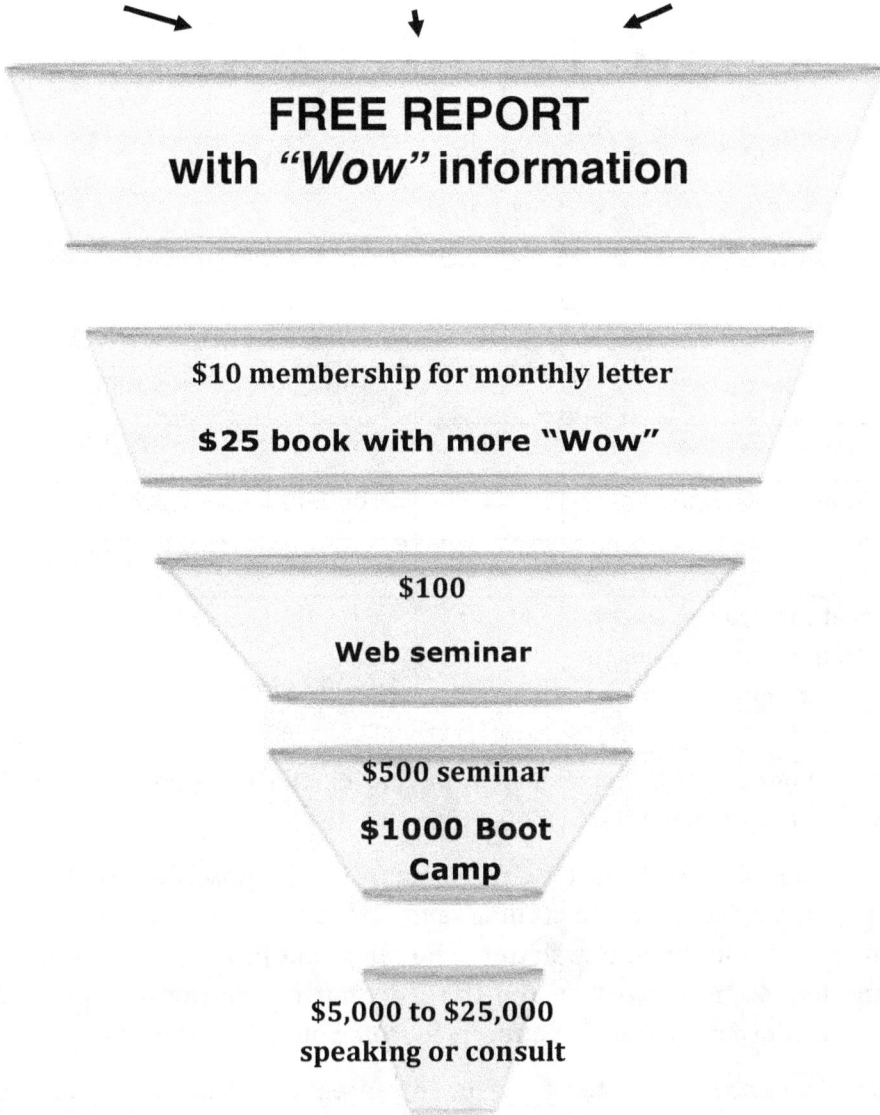

FREE REPORT
with *"Wow"* information

$10 membership for monthly letter

$25 book with more "Wow"

$100

Web seminar

$500 seminar

$1000 Boot Camp

$5,000 to $25,000 speaking or consult

$30,000 up front plus 30 percent of realized new profit for consulting or flat fee of $100,000 consulting fee

Let's plug some numbers into a chart so you can see the power of the funnel and the exponential growth possibility if you follow the steps as described.

The plan is very easy to implement; yet is very difficult for many to be disciplined enough to follow the plan as it is laid out.

The Funnel R.O.I

Offer	Subscriber	Investment	Revenue
FREE	1,000	$0.00	$ 0.00
Book	300	$30.00	$ 9,000.00
Webinar	100	$100.00	$ 10,000.00
Seminar	20	$500.00	$ 11,000.00
Speak/Consult	3	$5,000.00	$ 15,000.00
Immerse Consulting	1	$100,000.00	$ 100,000.00
		Total	$ 145,000.00
Repeat the process once a month in different cities for 12 months		Grand Total	$1,740,000.00

It is very important to be consistent in your email campaigns and monthly newsletters to achieve the $1,740,000 in twelve months.

Email a newsletter at least twice a month to all subscribers with some "Wow" information. Start a blog and interact with subscribers. The followers of your email newsletter, who might not pay for the second step of the funnel, may invest in the third or fourth step because of all the valuable information they have received from your e-newsletters.

What if you are committed to your entrepreneur business and promote your funnel system in four different cities at the same time each month? Then your end result in twelve months will be four times the above grand total. It will be $6,960,000.00 in one year. That is not bad for one year of commitment.

Create Your Funnel Plan

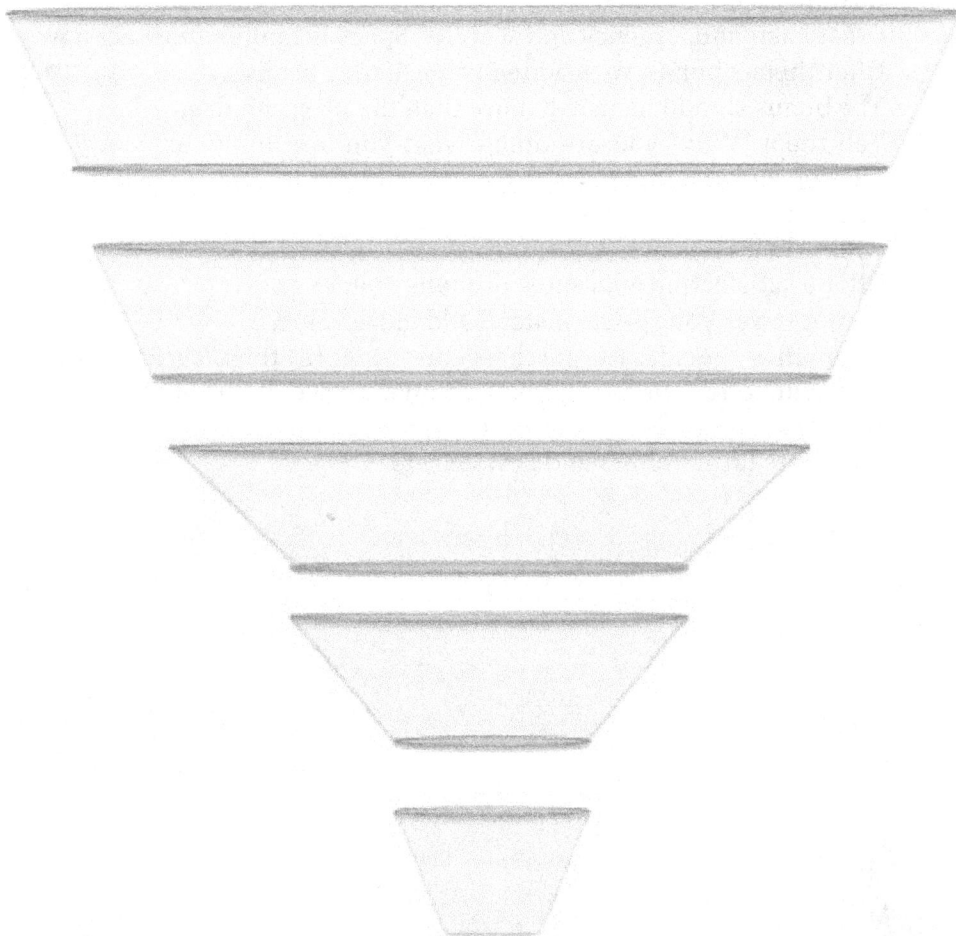

The Million-Dollar Conversion System

To increase the conversion rate of your audience, your presentation must include the following points to influence your audience to act now:

Offer them a free-gift with no commitment required from their part.

- Who are you? Why are you the expert in your field?
- Have testimonials for social proof and authority.
- Exploit the existing problem or challenge. Provide them with some "Wow" stats.

- Educate them on the cause of the problem. Provide them with "Wow" information.
- Give them your best out of the box strategies and solutions.
- Customers buy results.
- Create demand, urgency and scarcity. Space is limited must act now.
- Offer them a bonus, with added value, if they act now.
- The bonus should be worth more than the program itself.
- Tell them "Why" you are doing what you are doing. Explain your mission and vision.
- They have to connect to your "Why" to like you before they are willing to do business with you.
- Offer a satisfaction guarantee or money back.
- Do not lower your price; instead add more value.
- After they decide to purchase and before they click confirm payment, offer an up-sell for a lower price item, accessory or service.
- Automate future offers and newsletters.

CHAPTER 23

Linear vs. Residual Income

Linear Income

Most people work an average 9-to-5 job, where they go to work in the morning and come home at night, not worrying about their job until they go back to work the next morning. These people receive a paycheck at the end of the week based on how much work or how many hours they put in that week. They are basically trading their time for money, also known as linear income. If someone who receives linear income stops working, the money stops coming in. Linear income is true for more than 90 percent of people in the work force today. Is there a way to make money while you are not working? Wouldn't it be nice to wake up every morning with more money in your bank account? Although this doesn't seem possible at this moment, it is actually very possible. It is known as residual income.

Residual Income

Residual income is a much better and more powerful source of income and it is why the richest people in the world depend on this source of income. Most people trade time for money; rich people trade money for time. Successful entrepreneurs free themselves from the daily activities that don't generate money by hiring others to do the job. These entrepreneurs concentrate on innovating ways to draw more clients and money and on investing for the purpose of generating residual income. The idea behind residual income is that money keeps generating on a regular basis whether you are working at the time or not. Residual income is generally available to business owners and investors, people who make money even when they are not at work. This is because business owners have other people work for them, making money for them even when they are not present; while investors use their money to invest in high yield returns and have their money work for them.

There are four types of trade, which generate either linear or residual income:

Employees—invest time for money 9-5, five days a week
Self-employed—invest time for money 9-5, five to seven days a week
Business owners—invest other people's time for money 9-5, seven days a week
Entrepreneurs and investors—invest other people's time and money to make money twenty-four hours, seven days a week

Business Owners

Business owners are similar to the self-employed with a few big differences. Although the self-employed are technically business owners, the self-employed do the majority of the work themselves to earn money. Business owners have workers doing the majority of the work for the business. Successful business owners delegate the day to day tasks to focus more on how to expand the business and how they will reach that goal.

Investors and Entrepreneurs

Investors are entrepreneurs who have money, service or products working for them by making residual income! Successful entrepreneurs wake up every morning wealthier than the day before. They invest in different opportunities that provide residual income such as commercial and residential real estate properties, people with million dollar ideas, and discount notes, stocks and bonds. They receive residual income from licensing their products or services, writing books, blogging, selling monthly recurring memberships or franchising their business. They develop on line stores to sell worldwide with an automated marketing system to turn prospects to buyers.

Although everyone has different goals and skills in life, everyone should strive to become an investor.

Business owners and the self-employed should ask, "How can I turn a major part of my business into residual income?"

Can you start a membership program, where you collect money on a monthly basis regardless of whether clients use your services or not? Can you automate any service or sale procedure that generates money on a regular basis? Can you license your system to similar business to increase profit? Can you write a book to teach others how to duplicate your success?

If you purchase the property where your business is located then every rent payment reduces the mortgage payment and increases your assets value. Not to mention that every morning you will be waking up richer as the property you purchased appreciates in value. The goal is to work hard, then make residual income for a lifetime from what you created.

Generate Income **Invest**

Pay Yourself First to Earn a Million Dollars

We live in a disposable economy. If it is broken don't fix it, replace it! New is always better! Must keep up with the Jones! Most people are trained to buy a new house, new car, new everything every few years. An average person can't wait for the new iPhone to replace his perfectly functioning iPhone. Because of those habits, the average person has too many days left at the end of the month and not enough money. What you keep, not what you earn, is the indication whether or not you will become a millionaire. Learn to pay toward your investments first. To earn a million dollars, all you have to do is pay yourself first. It's amazing how a small investment of ten dollars a day at 12 percent interest can grow to one million dollars in thirty years. The question is, can you cut your daily expenses by ten dollars a day to invest it toward your future?

Did you know that if your parents invested one dollar a day from the day that you were born at 10 percent interest and you continued to invest the one dollar a day until you reach the age of retirement, the total investment would be two million, seven hundred thousand dollars?

Invest Less When You Invest Early

Because of the magic of compound interest, everyone should start investing early. Look at the chart below. Investors A and B are twin brothers who both invested in a tax-deferred account at 12 percent interest. Investor A started his investment at age 24. Investor B started the same IRA investment at age 30.

Investor A				Investor B	
Started investing at age 24				Started investing at age 30	
Age	Investment	End of year		Investment	End of year
24	$2,000.00	$2,240.00		$0.00	$0.00
25	$2,000.00	$4,479.00		$0.00	$0.00
26	$2,000.00	$7,559.00		$0.00	$0.00
27	$2,000.00	$10,706.00		$0.00	$0.00
28	$2,000.00	$14,230.00		$0.00	$0.00
29	$2,000.00	$18,178.00		$0.00	$0.00
30	$0.00	$20,359.00		$2,000.00	$2,240.00
31	$0.00	$22,803.00		$2,000.00	$4,479.00
32	$0.00	$25,539.00		$2,000.00	$7,559.00
33	$0.00	$28,603.00		$2,000.00	$10,706.00
34	$0.00	$32,036.00		$2,000.00	$14,230.00
35	$0.00	$35,880.00		$2,000.00	$18,178.00
36	$0.00	$40,186.00		$2,000.00	$20,359.00
37	$0.00	$45,008.00		$2,000.00	$22,803.00
38	$0.00	$50,409.00		$2,000.00	$25,539.00
39	$0.00	$56,458.00		$2,000.00	$28,603.00
40	$0.00	$63,233.00		$2,000.00	$32,036.00
45	$0.00	$111,438.00		$2,000.00	$95,767.00
50	$0.00	$196,393.00		$2,000.00	$183,005.00
55	$0.00	$346,111.00		$2,000.00	$336,748.00
60	$0.00	$609,966.00		$2,000.00	$607,695.00
64	$0.00	**$959,793.00**		$2,000.00	**$966,926.00**
Total	$12,000.00			$70,000.00	

Investor A deposited $2000 a year in his tax-deferred account for six years only, from age 24 to age 29 then he ceased, making a total investment of $12,000. Investor B waited six more years until he reached the age 30 to open his tax-deferred account. For the next 35 years he deposited $2000 a year in his tax-deferred account for a total of $70,000 investment. The result is at age sixty-five they both had nearly one million dollars in their retirement account.

> *"The secret of retiring as a millionaire is to be consistent in your investment and start early."*

Rituals and Goals

Stop everything you are doing. Find a pen and write on the left side of the chart below all your daily rituals then on the right side write all your goals.

Rituals	Goals

Now ask yourself does every ritual you wrote help you achieve your goals?

If not then go back to the chart and cross out the word *Rituals* and replace it with the word **Rich-uals** then cross out every previous ritual that does not contribute to achieving your goals and replace it with a new one. If you want to achieve your goals, you must work on these rich-uals every day and give them priority over other daily practices.

Just by asking you three questions I can predict your future:

1- What books do you read?
2- Do you have a mentor?
3- Who are the people you spend most of your time with?

By you reading this book, I know what kind of books you read.

Do you have at least one mentor? Who is your mentor? Your mentor must be someone who already achieved way beyond your dream. Your mentor will hold you accountable and laser focus on your goals.

Who are the friends you spend most of your time with? Who are your friends you network with? Would your current friends hold you down or will they help you achieve your dreams and goals?

One Single Action Can Double Your Income

What if there were one action you could take to put you on the road to double your income? Would you do it? First look at these stats.

• According to the Economic Research Division of the Federal Reserve Bank, the average American works about 32.76 hours per week.
• According to Nielson numbers, the average American watches 34 hours of television per week.

If you want to double your income then turn the television off and do something productive in order to reach your financial goals.

From Local to Global

Because we live in a global economy, we need to shift our thinking from local to global. Otherwise we will be missing out on some great opportunities.

When a brick and mortar business operates locally, they search for a good location in an office building or shopping center. They also research local demographics, traffic count in front of their business, and foot traffic which they depend on to generate profits. On top of that, they have to pay rent and all business expenses and liabilities necessary to operate.

On the other hand, all e-commerce businesses have the same great location. If you promote on-line, on the appropriate sites that are geared towards the type of customers you are looking for, you will have more traffic on your Internet location than at any physical location.

Search engines filter what type of customers you are looking for. Anytime someone surfs the web, Google, for instance, keeps track of their searching and buying habits, and will push ads of interest to them.

Can you take your business from local to global?

If you have a service business, you can start a blog filled with knowledge that will benefit the consumer, and you can become an expert in your field. You can also have a premium membership for your followers so they can receive a monthly newsletter with "Wow" information.

With good traffic, some major companies will approach you and pay big bucks for advertising space on your blog.

- Become an expert of your niche market.
- Offer valuable information.
- Have a membership for your monthly letter. With a $40 membership fee and 1000 subscribers, you have: 1000 x $40 = $40,000 per month.
- Add Google ads to your blog. The more traffic you attract to your site, the more money you can make from ads. Your income from Google ads may exceed seven figures, depending on your blog traffic.
- Add affiliate programs to your site. It is a type of performance-based marketing in which a business rewards you for each visitor

or customer brought to them by clicking on their link from your website.

Can you transform your retail store from local to global?

Can a restaurant take advantage of the Internet and sell globally?

Can you promote your product or service in Europe as an American product? Many products used regularly in the United States are regularly are a scarcity in Europe and vice-versa. Once you decide to work globally, your front store becomes an e-commerce store. You will have the advantage over your existing physical location in every respect.

E-commerce is easy to start. As an Internet business you will

- Overcome geographic limitations.
- Have the whole world from which to choose your demographics.
- Reach global markets with more traffic from search engines.
- Attract more interested prospects to your site.
- Lower transaction costs.
- Be open for business twenty-four hours a day, seven days a week.
- Save your customers traveling time and shopping time.
- Allow customers a way to shop from the convenience of their homes.
- Add Google ads to your website for extra income.
- Entrepreneurs make at least 25 percent more money than the general population makes. Home-based businesses have more than double the success than brick and mortar businesses.

As an entrepreneur, it is easy to make millions of dollars. All you have to do is sell:

$1 widgets to 1 million people

$10 widgets to 100,000 people

$100 widgets to 10,000 people

$1000 widgets to 1000 people (sweet spot)

$10,000 widgets to 100 people

$100,000 widgets to 10 people

1 million dollar widget to 1 person

Gain The Unfair Advantage

There are many e-commerce businesses competing with you. Don't leave it to chance. You must have an unfair advantage for surfers to buy from you. Below are some ideas to use:

- Promote your UVP to separate yourself from the competition.
- Educate prospects rather than trying to sell them.
- Offer a risk free, money back guarantee.
- Remove barriers. Offer free shipping if possible.
- Start a blog.
- Be the expert in your niche market.
- Add pictures and video clips to your site.
- Promote your video clips on YouTube.
- Add new information to your e-commerce site regularly.
- Use a squeeze page to capture e-mail addresses.
- Give a free gift with opt-in email.
- Use an email marketing company.
- Automate offers or newsletter to your database.
- Hire a professional search engine optimization person.
- Hire a social media expert.
- Hire a virtual assistant.
- Hire a PR person.

> *"You don't have to be great to start,*
> *but you have to start to be great."*

You are not alone

As mentioned at the beginning of the book, the foundation for success starts with the following three elements:

- Read books daily to improve your skills and expand your mind.
- Network and mastermind with people who have common goals that will support you in your journey to success.
- Hire a mentor who has already achieved way beyond your goals and dreams to accelerate your success.

Contact AJ Rassamni if you need help with applying any of the above elements. AJ offers a membership program, Joint Venture Private Community, webinars, and one-on-one mentoring programs.

If you are stuck in your business and need help, or if you have a great idea and want to start a Joint Venture, or want to partner with AJ Rassamni, write to him via email and someone will respond to your request info@GainTheUnfairAdvantage.com

www.ingramcontent.com/pod-product-compliance
Lightning Source LLC
Chambersburg PA
CBHW051334200326
41519CB00026B/7424